Praise for *Be Human, Be Happy, Be YOU!*

I have known Raditia for many years and have been fascinated by the way she sees life. She's firm in her belief that everything in life has a purpose and that nothing occurs without reason. It is her approach to life that is so beautifully expressed in *Be Human, Be Happy, Be YOU!* which also reminds us to trust how life unfolds. Every moment is a puzzle piece needed to create a complete picture of our lives.

~ Stephanie Greter, Founder of yourSIGN, Switzerland

The book *Be Human, Be Happy, Be YOU!* by Raditia Lasry reflects her passion for the human experience. Her curiosity shines through her mindful approach to life. While pushing boundaries and cultural norms, Raditia provides thought-provoking and sometimes challenging ideas to create a life that doesn't always give simple or quick resolutions. She truly embodies her words, "taking life by the heart and following it." A worthwhile read for those curious about living a more mindful, meaningful life.

~ Lisa Kindle, Artist and Creator of the Color Affirmation Method, USA

If you want to learn about mindfulness in a practical, relatable way, this book is for you. Raditia gives you different perspectives on mindfulness and shares her story, her experience, her insights, and her learnings in carefully crafted chapters. Each chapter is a gem by itself and holds intimate anecdotes on what it means to be human and how we can navigate this journey with more joy and mindfulness.

~ Deadou Schaller, Yoga, Human Design & Meditation Coach, Switzerland

Learning to be honest with yourself is a vital lesson in life. Embrace being human and discover the art of being happy being yourself, as beautifully and inspiringly narrated by Raditia in her book *Be Human, Be Happy, Be YOU!*

> ~ Kristina Krieger, Educator and Mother of Three, Germany

Raditia is passionate about Mindfulness and has applied it to her own life in many ways, as she shares with the reader in *Be Human, Be Happy, Be YOU!* Her inspirational story takes us from her home in Switzerland to the United States, where she has made a life for herself as a coach and mentor to others seeking a more meaningful life experience. Yes, there will always be ups and downs in life, according to the author, but it is possible to be fulfilled and happy.

> ~ Valerie Block, Retiree, USA

Be Human, Be Happy, Be YOU! is a remarkable book that recounts the journey of an exceptional author through the highs and lows of life. The author candidly and touchingly shares her personal stories of overcoming numerous obstacles. In moments of crisis and doubt, she demonstrates how she grew through the challenges, ultimately finding a more fulfilling life through mindfulness.

These are stories that touch the heart and impart wisdom that prompts the reader to reflect. The author unfolds her own transformation, illustrating how she rose from difficulties to reach a place of inner peace and self-acceptance. In doing so, she builds a bridge between her experiences and the possibilities that mindfulness offers to discover happiness and authenticity.

This book is more than just an autobiography; it is an invitation to join the journey. The author encourages the

reader to embark on their own path, viewing obstacles as opportunities and setting out to lead a more conscious and fulfilling life. *Be Human, Be Happy, Be YOU!* is a valuable source of inspiration for anyone seeking personal growth and inner harmony. Immerse yourself in this moving narrative that not only reveals the power of mindfulness but also encourages contemplation of one's uniqueness and the pursuit of an authentic and joyful life.
~ Christine Hegglin, Founder and Owner of Hegglin Group AG and hoyou.ch, Switzerland

Raditia is the kind of teacher you want to learn from. It is apparent that her teachings are derived from her lived experiences, forged in the crucible of daily living. Her stories are alive, transparent, and full of insights that only come from years of studying and being with oneself. *Be Happy, Be Human, Be YOU!* is a book that you will read more than once. Every time you revisit it will yield new wisdom for you to continually apply to your life and journey as you grow in your own mindful being.
~ Daniel Allen, Speaker, Digital Educator, Entrepreneur, USA

Be Human, Be Happy, Be YOU!

A journey finding inner lightness, freedom, and ease

Be Human, Be Happy, Be YOU!

A journey finding inner
lightness, freedom, and ease

Raditia

HenschelHAUS Publishing, Inc.
Milwaukee, Wisconsin

Copyright © 2024 by Raditia Lasry
All rights reserved.

Published by
HenschelHAUS Publishing, Inc.
Milwaukee, Wisconsin
www.henschelHAUSbooks.com

Cover photo by the author.
Sunset on Kauai, Hawaii (April 2019)

Author photo by Sonja Andenmatten

ISBN (hardcover) 978159598-985-7
ISBN (paperback) 978159598-986-4
LCCN: 2024930514

Printed in the United States of America

Dedication

To my family, parents, and friends who allowed
me to become the person I am today.

Table of Contents

Preface	i
Why Mindfulness?	1
Introduction	5
Life Discoveries	11
Flow of Life	35
My Love	47
Me, My Child, & Mindfulness	63
Living and Dying	81
Lessons Learned	99
Mindful Being	125
Unconditional Love	143
11 Attitudes of Mindfulness	177
Conclusion	207
Acknowledgments	211
Resources and Recommended Reading	217
About the Author	219

Preface

The life we live has become full of uncertainty worldwide and at home in health, jobs, and relationships.

Wherever we turn, we find new challenges to overcome. When will it stop? When will we be free of struggles? I don't have the answers to those questions. What I do have is how we can find inner lightness, freedom, and ease with everything that's being thrown at us by recognizing our humanness. This journey starts as an inside job—something we all have access to and often disregard, resist, and mistrust.

This book is here to bring awareness to our past, present, and future by welcoming all parts of us: our body, mind, emotions, perceptions, and points of view. I provide different perspectives on everyday experiences we encounter and often overlook as they seem mundane and unnecessary.

In the following pages, I reflect on my own life experiences and integrate various possibilities on how

Be Human, Be Happy, Be YOU!

we can still be happy and embrace being ourselves in a world that requires us to fit in and that constantly changes.

The challenges I faced were mainly in the realm of social, professional, and educational structures. At first, I felt limited by those structures. Once I cracked the code that I am the creator of my life, my shackles of being the victim fell off. I started to see opportunities where there were limitations. I found deeper connections where once there were disconnects.

My hope is that this book will support you in your daily life to bring more joy and ease to you and the people around you. One thing no one can take away from you is who you are.

~ Raditia

Why Mindfulness?

When I started writing this book, I was in the beginning phase of my dedicated journey of walking on the path of mindfulness.

Before I share with you how the path evolved, let's begin by answering the question: what is mindfulness? Mindfulness has many definitions. My favorite version is:

Being present with what is without judgment.

As I write this phrase and reflect on what mindfulness meant at the begining of my journey, my vantage point has expanded. Even though the foundation has remained the same, I now better understand why I have committed my work to mindfulness.

Becoming a mother was easy at first. I was blessed to have a son who was quiet, easy-going, and loved traveling. Once he turned two and was able to resist my urgency to leave the house on time, I discovered my limits of being a calm and collected parent.

Be Human, Be Happy, Be YOU!

Becoming a parent required an additional foundation and practice that could help me move through life with more ease and gracefully handle any challenges still ahead of me.

Something in me needed attention. Something in me felt I had to change the person I was. A few months before, I had lost my job and decided to get a degree in the United States. I was born in Switzerland, and not having a *standard American* education led to some challenges when I first arrived in New York in 2003.

I realize now that I looked more deeply into the practice of mindfulness because I loved who I was. And today, I love the energetic, emotional, and loving person that I am.

Another reason I am writing this book is because I want to express how simple and supportive life can be and show that we are the ones who make life difficult. The practice of mindfulness allows us to explore all the ups and downs with less urgency and more agency. I see mindfulness as the groundwork of being human.

Why Mindfulness?

Thich Nhat Hanh describes mindfulness as *the art of living*. With all the challenges we face and witness from war, climate change, political and economic difficulties, and how we interact with one another, and especially with ourselves, we need practices that support us along the way.

Some might see mindfulness as foreign and with a spiritual touch. Others might see it as a tool to cope with stress. Yet others could understand it solely as meditation. All of the mentioned aspects are true to some extent. However, there is more to mindfulness as well. I would love for you to discover this journey of mindfulness as one way of developing unconditional love for yourself and finding joy in living now. Indeed, mindfulness teaches us how to be human.

Reflecting on how mindfulness threaded its way through my life, I have also noticed that it's a breakthrough of generational conditioning and social construct. As I share my journey—from my relationships with my parents and brother, my spouse and my son—and creating an extended

Be Human, Be Happy, Be YOU!

relationship with myself, I invite you to explore this journey for yourself.

And as the title of this book states, the moment we embrace being human with all the quirks and ups and downs, we begin to live happily and, above all, be ourselves.

Introduction

Where do I begin? Before writing the book you hold in your hands, I had written an entirely different version of this book three years prior. That book was also about my journey, more of a chronicle and included all the details about how I got to the United States. As I reread it and wanted to continue writing and completing the book, I felt disconnected from what I had written, even though it all was true and my story. I had described my life from an intellectual side and not from what I know best—my emotional and heart-centered side.

While I was growing up and even today, I feel my emotions and, more often than not, also express them. My greatest evolution—from when I was little to my current age of 44—is how I relate to my feelings.

Some summers ago, several people commented on how much my previously confrontational personality had calmed down. Much has happened over the years and people found my changes noticeable.

My emotions brought me to mindfulness. My challenge was not my inability to express them but rather to share them in a way that people would hear what I was saying and still want to connect with me.

I used to express myself reactively—my version of a cry for help—though nobody seemed to hear me. Additionally, I practiced letting out my emotions so much that it had become a comfort zone. It was a release mechanism to avoid hosting any unresolved issues within. Even today, I want to resolve things immediately, even when the problem or difficulty is my fault. I don't want to hold disruptions inside.

I also started to understand that as an outsider, the other person, it is not always easy to fully comprehend what is going on or to determine if a discussion is based on something underlying or not. By understanding what is happening below the surface, we might be able to avoid future outbreaks and discomfort.

The discussion could be about something simple, like recurring activities, such as taking out the

Introduction

garbage or washing the dishes. Perhaps the underlying issue is that we are seeking greater equality in a relationship. Or perhaps we feel overwhelmed and haven't found the best way to communicate our daily struggles, and therefore take our frustration or even anger out on others.

Throughout my life, I have felt challenged for a variety of reasons. One aspect, a common one, is that as a child, I wanted more attention and love from my parents than I was receiving. Looking back now and discovering what love means, much has changed. While growing up, we focused on what parents and teachers were thinking and expressing, excluding our emotions at an early age. We have learned that such supression can harm everyone involved, especially later in life. Those emotions can resurface in new experiences, not realizing that they are based in childhood. We do not live in an environment that always understands why our emotions get intense.

Receiving the help we need can be tricky when an underlying, unmet feeling exists. There is a significant chance we will express our discomfort and

Be Human, Be Happy, Be YOU!

dismay in misunderstood ways and add more labels to something they are not.

Looking closely at what we give our attention to daily, it's the love we seek in all forms. We are looking for appreciation, recognition, acknowledgment, thank you's, and other gestures indicating that someone we give our attention to cares for our actions and presence. And yet, often, we don't get such acknowledgement in the ways we are seeking.

In my case, when I was a teenager, I was energetic and even feisty about expressing my unmet needs. I didn't recognize my impact or my intentions. My tantrums or outbursts were solely to make myself feel better about myself and, in some ways, get love from others. These actions didn't always work out well and most times, I didn't receive the love I sought.

I am sharing this because as I listen to people's experiences and expressions today, we all seek love in a way that we don't usually get in return. We always wish our parents would express their love this way and wonder, "Why can't they say or do things the way I need them to?" Perhaps we become unable to

Introduction

hear what they are actually saying and misinterpret what we want our loved ones to say. We end up in a never-ending cycle of unmet needs.

I have written this book to demonstrate how we can determine what we are truly looking for. From whom and where can we find the love? And though you might already know the answer, it will take a lifetime of practice and reminders. I call it unconditional love towards ourselves or simply "being human."

Once we recognize and embody that love for ourselves, loving others becomes a piece of cake—even strangers and people who we find more difficult to love—and start loving them like our children and pets.

Life Discoveries

I'll begin this journey with the "expected" love between me and my parents. This relationship is the most significant one in our lives and is the one that can determine many of our future connections to people and perspectives. How we are raised can define how we respond and react to our life challenges. Often, our reactions happen so subconsciously that it is necessary to build strong and trusting relationships, bonds that can inform us about how people notice us. We live in such bubbles that if we didn't have conflicts and challenges with other people, we would never know how our past plays a role in our present.

Learning about what it means to be human can be very freeing and supportive. Why? Because in our society, what we describe as our focuses and jobs are generally far away from what it actually means to be alive. Therefore, we often distance ourselves from what makes us truly happy and what it takes to be ourselves.

Be Human, Be Happy, Be YOU!

* * *

Early on, probably before my teens, I realized the impact my parents had on me. I fought my way through with no luck. I wanted them to see what I saw, yet they were not able to. I felt lonely and almost hopeless. There was even a particular moment when I wasn't able to see a reason for living. It was in an argument with my mother. I can't recall the details; I hadn't gotten what I wanted or had some other disagreement. I gathered up all my money and as I approached the door, I said something to her that was followed by, "I'm leaving, and I won't come back." Her response was "Go ahead. There's the door."

Something happened in that moment. I can't say what it was. My mother taught me an important lesson. I realized that this was my life to live. When I played with the thought of putting an end to my life, I realized I wouldn't achieve anything. I therefore changed what was important to me. I focused on friends and connections, even when it meant not achieving good grades.

Life Discoveries

That situation was also the beginning of finding myself in an internal conflict between what the outside world expected and seemed essential and what I, my little inside, wanted to focus on. I did my best to do both while staying true to myself and meeting the needs of others, and at the same time, I didn't succeed. That subconsciously paved my way to mindfulness.

There was another moment. Again, I don't recall the exact details, but I was walking by myself. I didn't feel accepted by my classmates or the people in my environment. I told myself, "No matter what, I'll be happy." That became my focus—to do whatever it took to be happy, not realizing why mindfulness ended up on my path. At the beginning, when I focused on making mindfulness my path, I came across a quote by Thich Nhat Hanh that says, "Mindfulness is a source of happiness." It all started to make sense.

* * *

These life-changing experiences are a reminder to keep discovering and learning that there is much more to the story than black and white. There is actually a lot of gray.

How we can lead to more gray is by noticing how often we use "or" and other subconscious, automated responses that limit our possibilities. There is a lot of both/and. There are sayings and sentences we use like "black or white," "all or nothing," "right or wrong," "good or bad." And what if it's not either/or but both/and?

By becoming aware of our tendencies and habits, we reach the core of mindfulness. By the way, we all carry the gift of mindfulness. What happened along the way is that we automated our lives and did our best to simplify things. That provides us with more time for the other things that we want to pay more attention to.

Although the aspects of mindfulness are in the intention to simplify, if we live in a more automated way than not, we are also missing out on the precious moment of "now" and the impact of living in the moment has on our life, the primary purpose of this book.

Let's remind ourselves how precious our lives

Life Discoveries

truly are. We spend a lot of time dissatisfied with specific experiences and miss the silver lining, whether it's in traffic, having rainy and cold days, having conflicts with a loved one, and many other experiences we consider negative. Notice those moments for what they are and not for what they seem to be.

We must condition our minds to be more aware of celebratory moments rather than getting caught up in the things that don't work out. Throughout this book, I'll share different experiences—from having a child and losing a loved one to how life presents us with challenges. How can we begin to see the rainbows in our lives rather than only viewing things in black and white?

* * *

There are two sides to mindfulness. Let's use the example of a dove and its two wings—one wing is **awareness** and the other wing is **remembering**. This imagery is taken from a mindfulness training taught by Tara Brach.[1] The older we get, the more difficult it is to change our daily habits and automated thought processes.

Be Human, Be Happy, Be YOU!

Let's begin with awareness. Any changes we want to make will only happen if we are aware and observant of what is going on and where our minds are. And unless we are willing to change because something in our lives isn't working out the way we hoped, we will not make those changes.

Only a few of us will pick up a new hobby and habit to our busy schedule if it is optional. If you are not interested, and it doesn't provide you with any rewards, then you would not be investing your time and money.

If you get added awareness from reading this book, that will make me happy. If you are intrigued by making mindfulness a way of living by the time you finish this book, that would be amazing, too. At the end of the day, my stories are not the relevant message. What matters is *YOUR* story and how you can make your life what you want it to be while embracing all its facets.

Once we have full awareness of most of our actions, we are more likely to add the second wing of **remembering**. We will have established a few ways of remembering how our habits and tendencies affect us and the people around us.

Life Discoveries

There are undiscussed aspects of expectations of life and other people. For instance, the expectation of earning a degree after studying, focusing on success and wealth, keeping our emotions to ourselves, and believing happiness is based on external circumstances.

The majority of people live within such expectations. Then there are people who want to make a mark by recognizing the importance of showing up for their troubled and perhaps difficult experiences. People of minorities, such as race, culture, religion, ethnicity, sexual orientation, educational accessibility, and many other facets, are fighting the status quo and raising awareness of their experiences so that they can create a new future for themselves and, more importantly, plant seeds for those who follow in their footsteps.

In my mindfulness teacher training with Tara Brach and Jack Kornfield, they added a program about Diversity, Equity, Inclusivity, and Accessibility (DEIA). During that time, I discovered the inner-life challenges I had while growing up. I noticed the experience of being different because of my upbringing and cultural background, which led to different thought processes and how they affect me.

I know I am not alone. Every one of us experiences moments of non-belonging, loneliness, discovering differences with our mates, and doing anything to fit in, be it financially, culturally, politically, religiously, racially, educationally, and for some other reason.

There were—and still are—moments where I feel pressured to be something I am not. Only now do I realize that truly being ourselves is one of the characteristics that we as humans are mainly challenged by. As a society, we are unable to embrace the billions of different people living on this earth. It is impossible to create structures and regulations that fit everyone's needs. The longer we exist on this earth, the more people will reside on this planet, the more variety and differences we will discover, and the more challenging it will get to meet all our needs.

This book isn't here to tell you not to pursue activism with regard to a mission you are passionate about and want to make a difference in. This book is here to give you a practice that can support you on this challenging journey called life. Mindfulness is one way to embrace all the struggles we encounter on our path and find the way to ourselves. To create a place within ourselves that we carry with us and that will remain a safe place no matter what environment or situation in which we find ourselves.

Mindfulness can be the guide when moments of worldly uproar and human rights are violated. My passion and mission are for humans to be at peace with what is, to make choices that support themselves and the greater good for the future, and to move with their fears in a way that doesn't harm others only because we don't know how to handle them. We can learn by watching and observing other cultures.

The bottom line is that we all want to be happy and at peace at the end of the day. The measurements of how society accepts our decisions and abilities—education, vocation, relationships—sometimes don't include everyone. Most of the time, we only have the capacity to pay attention to our own needs—something I noticed even when I was a child.

Be Human, Be Happy, Be YOU!

The only way we can make the world a place of connections and love is by beginning to love ourselves more. We struggle to be receptive and caring because our ancient brains were trained to look out for danger to keep us safe. We need more practice differentiating the danger we are looking at these days. The danger we see today is danger in a relational, financial, and professional way. There is much less danger of saving our lives from wild animals, at least most of the time.

In these moments, I notice how we need additional practice and investigation about ourselves and humans in general. We don't get enough time and resources to discover how we affect and are affected by one another. Indeed, the practice of mindfulness is one of the leading resources that can support us on this journey of discovering ourselves.

These perspectives of mindfulness need repeating:

- Mindfulness never judges us.
- It always meets us with open arms, no matter what we do.

Life Discoveries

- It lets us see ourselves and others with kindness and compassion.
- It listens and increases our trust.

How do I practice mindfulness when life sends me curveballs and I find myself on a rollercoaster? This question might come up through an illness, the passing of a loved one, losing a job, or waking up on the wrong side of the bed.

It's time to look at what is in front of us. There are times I struggle with making mindfulness an accessible pathway, with all the suffering and struggles we can face in our lifetimes. There are so many ways we can harm ourselves and each other.

As I embark on this journey of sharing my ideas and ways of living a complete life, please note that I might say or write things that don't reflect your experience. When you notice that those thoughts, sensations, and emotions arise, take a moment and acknowledge your experience. See if you can meet your experience without judgment.

As the *Serenity Prayer* states: "Grant me the serenity to accept the things I cannot change, the courage to change the things I can, and the wisdom to know the difference."

In certain moments of our lives, we have choices. Sometimes, we don't. We encounter experiences especially related to health, where we often are not given a choice. And more often than not, we don't realize what our choices are. We can't put the sole blame on the government and the societal structures that are put into place to make society work for all of us.

What I discovered in the past year as we witness the many challenges from political, sexual, racial, cultural, and other suppressing actions, there are ways we can make a difference. What I am about to say isn't **THE** way; it's *A* way to move through these challenges. You might have guessed it—mindfulness is *A* way.

In our everyday lives, we blame others and even things because we don't like that feeling of being wrong and making mistakes. What I have noticed, especially in the day and age in which we find ourselves, with easy access to technology—such as digital devices and their perks and unlimited ways to connect to the outside world—it is very easy to get distracted. When we are distracted, we don't focus well. Maybe we're even multitasking, making it much easier to make mistakes. With all we are exposed to, and what we need to attend to, it is even more important to excel in the skills of paying attention and ultimately, mindfulness.

Mindfulness is the practice of paying attention to what we are doing in a particular moment, free of judgment.

When we have tools like autocorrect, it would be helpful to pay more attention to what is being corrected. The other day, I saw someone use the following sentence in their signature of an email: "Typos not my fault." Okay, it might be a joke, yet, at the same time, isn't that giving away ownership of our actions? This is just one example, and I am sure there are many other situations in which we blame something or someone else right off the bat.

Another example I can think of in a different scenario is when we are running late to get somewhere. That's when the traffic lights go against us, there is traffic where there is never any, or someone pulls in front of us and makes us miss the light. We want to believe that those occurrences are someone else's fault. When we are honest with ourselves, our actions (of running late) led us to be at a particular place at a later time. Sometimes running late can also be a blessing in disguise because we might have avoided an accident. All I want to point out here is that we're not making the situation any better by blaming someone or something else for the consequences that impact us.

I have learned that the more honest we can become with ourselves and the actions or non-actions we are taking, the easier it becomes to take responsibility for our actions and allow others to do the same. Life becomes easier because we don't focus so much on avoiding mistakes and instead focus on what we are doing. And the best part: fewer mistakes will happen.

I also want to take a closer look at distractions, mainly because they are what we are up against. With all the beautiful tools we created and evolved into, the more aware we need to become. It is a necessity

Life Discoveries

these days. If we neglect this vital aspect when we are at the mercy of practicing awareness, life will pass us by. We will miss incredible moments of our children, loved ones, and even strangers. I find the extensive use of our digital devices frightening.

As I was writing this, I was sitting in a park and witnessing a couple walking together, both on their cell phones. From what I observed, there were moments when both did something individually, and there were moments when they connected and discussed something on the phone, and a third scenario when one person was talking while, the other one was focused on their phone.

I am sure this is a familiar scene. I am confident we have all been there. Often, we do multiple things simultaneously, from walking, talking, and texting with someone, even while watching TV. Without judging these actions, I want to highlight what we're actually doing—only giving partial attention to each other and our settings. We might comment: "I heard everything you said; I was here with you." Yet, were we really?

Be Human, Be Happy, Be YOU!

Ask yourself the next time when you attend to multiple things at once. Are you paying equal attention to all the things you are doing? If you answered yes, I am not so sure. According to how our brain functions, it's impossible for our brain to focus on multiple things at the same time. Even though it makes us feel like we are getting more things done, if we could practice focusing on one thing we're doing, we could get our tasks done faster, with fewer mistakes, with greater efficiency, and accomplish more overall than if we were switching between tasks every 45 to 60 seconds.

Just think of the number of times we let ourselves get distracted by our phones while driving, at work, and even with friends and family.

What if we gave our full attention to what we're actually doing? We would not have to blame others as much, and the best thing is we would live a fuller life. And yes, it would mean we have to practice saying "no." We would not be able to do it all. And would it be so bad to get more connection and love for what we do?

Life Discoveries

We have trained and conditioned ourselves to deliver, provide, and increase productivity at the price of our bodies, mind, and the people we love. We have come to believe that disregarding our body's request for rest is a price we are willing to pay for success. Taking a break doesn't need to be 20 minutes; it can be as brief as

- leaning back in a chair,
- possibly closing your eyes,
- not holding a phone or listening to something or someone, and
- just being aware of our body, emotions, sensations, and thoughts for a few deep breaths.

What happens when we are sick? When loved ones pass away? Or when life takes a turn? How will we remember the days that have passed already? Isn't it in our interest to create valuable experiences and live as long as possible? What if living a fulfilling life means starting to do less and paying more attention to what's right in front of us—the people we love and the work we attend to.

Be Human, Be Happy, Be YOU!

Even if we think, "I only do my job so I can pay my bills," most of our waking hours will be spent at work. What if we could make those experiences not just a grind but part of our lives, we could live fully and intentionally, even if that might mean not enjoying all the tasks and not completing many of our to-dos.

No matter what, our to-do list will only get longer, not shorter. By realizing this and being honest about filling our plates too full, we will do what we can and pay attention to what's right in front of us and not feel guilty about the undone tasks. Instead, we could celebrate what we were able to accomplish.

I am not here to change your job. I am here to present you with how amazing life is. I'm sharing my story to make our lives more effortless and let you see what parts of your life you might not have paid much attention to. What did you miss while looking at your phone and not giving yourself a breather?

The following pages will show how you can make a difference by looking at life differently, without changing the life you're living. See how you can be the creator of your life with what you have in a way that gets your life back.

I can't tell you how much joy it can bring when we stop seeing problems and start seeing solutions. Life becomes so much more than what we thought it was. And talking about thoughts, we can pick what thoughts we want to attend to. Unfortunately, our brain isn't preselecting which thoughts are helpful and which should be disregarded. We have to do the work of becoming aware of our thoughts and choosing what thoughts are beneficial in a particular moment. It is in our own interest to give our full attention and make awareness and presence our main practice if we want to look back at life with gratitude and no regrets.

Mindfulness is a complex topic because it includes our whole being (brain, nervous system, thoughts, emotions, etc.). It encompasses all the past experiences of our lives, as well as the ones of our ancestors, all the different environments we have been and are in, and everything we come in touch with.

Be Human, Be Happy, Be YOU!

Mindfulness is not something you'll achieve or understand by reading this or numerous other books. It only comes with the lived experience of trial and error. The more we practice and try what works and doesn't work, the greater our success will be. Mindfulness never fails us. Although it doesn't pay our bills, it can give some ease to the restlessness and urges of life. With enough patience and less forcing, we will find creative ways to make life happen for us.

Practicing mindfulness might mean changing our focus from more to less. Each of us experiences life differently with all the challenges, struggles, and sufferings we face.

I have also recognized that we only know the world we live in. We can never know what others are going through, even if they share every detail of their journey. As I share my story, you might see your reflection and recognize similar situations, yet your experience will differ. You will see the value of your life experiences, and that's where we move from.

When we find things that make us happy, let's keep going. If things worry us and hold us back, we must find the courage to look those things in the eye and see if we can make a change.

One simple way to demonstrate moving forward even when life isn't easy is by introducing the eleven mindfulness attitudes set forth by Christiane Wolf, MD, Ph.D., and J. Greg Serpa, Ph.D., in the book *A Clinician's Guide to Teaching Mindfulness*. Initially, seven of these attitudes were established by Jon Kabat Zinn. In the last chapter of this book, I will explore them in more detail because they are a haven for our life's experiences and how we can support ourselves when life is taking a toll on us or we are showing signs of overwhelm.

Exploring the eleven fundamental attitudes of mindfulness gives us a foundation of where to begin and where we can always return:

1. Curiosity
2. Kindness
3. Gratitude & Generosity
4. Acceptance
5. Non-judgment
6. Non-striving

Be Human, Be Happy, Be YOU!

7. Letting go and letting be
8. Patience
9. Humor
10. Trust
11. A Beginner's Mind

The beauty of these attitudes is that if we work on one, we will automatically take care of the others. When we practice and move through our challenges, we want to pick one that suits the situation we're in. I'll go into more depth later on with an example for each attitude.

A twelfth attitude will be cultivated as we care for the eleven attitudes, which is ***compassion***. The way compassion increases is by learning how to use any of the eleven attitudes to move from feeling pity for ourselves to a more supportive thought-encouraging, solution-oriented, and forward-moving notion, which won't let us sit in misery for too long but will find a way to be with what is with more ease and look for ways to improve our situation.

When we can practice a beginner's mind with ourselves, we will soon be viewing other people's

Life Discoveries

obstacles as possible opportunities to move into a more encouraging and caring environment. There, we can meet others with compassion and invite them to see their situation with an optimistic outlook.

There have been many different stages in my life where I have established a certain sense of mindfulness. One of my cultivated mindfulness practices is bringing a smile to my lips even in challenging times.

Throughout this book, I'd like to bring sunshine into your life by encouraging you to care for yourself, to get to know yourself with all the likes and dislikes, and to establish unity with the people around you.

By bringing a smile to my face and hopefully one to yours, I am building my own foundation in practicing mindfulness and making it my mission and passion to share it with more people. Thank you for joining this journey with me.

Endnote

[1] www.tarabrach.com

Flow of Life

I had already finished the first draft of this book when I realized I needed to include a chunk of life's evolution. So many events and outcomes occurred because I lived from one moment to the next. Let me share how some events came together.

When we let life happen, for the most part, we will be surprised and gifted with why we are on this earth in the first place, not because we already know how it all will turn out.

Before I go into my personal take on the flow of life, let's discuss a recent and tremendous curveball—COVID. We had to figure out life on a daily basis. It was clear that people had their own individual challenges with how to move with this new reality.

How was the COVID experience for you? Were you able to take each day as it evolved? Did you find yourself in a frenzy, not knowing how or where to continue? What challenges did you face? What are your takeaways and lessons learned?

Be Human, Be Happy, Be YOU!

My personal take on the past few years is that the restrictions and fears felt like a lifetime. Once we became more used to the situation and got over its novelty, I was not able to tell time. Sometimes I couldn't remember if something happened two years or five years ago. However, for the most part, my experience was great. I was able to fully explore my practice of "Flow of Life," taking each day as it presented itself.

Those COVID days were a perfect practice of mindfulness and demonstrated the decades of practice needed to move daily with more ease. I would like to share with you how certain moments in my life without a specific goal or outcome turned into unforgettable moments that led me to the next unexpected moment.

Over the years, I learned that life is also a way to integrate humanness. I believe that is a significant piece that allows happiness to surprise us because our bodies, brains, and minds are in constant movement, hence flow.

Here are a few examples in which the circumstances could not have been planned.

Flow of Life

One of the instances that impacted my life, where one thing led to another, is how I ended up in the United States, New York City to be exact, and the people I've met along the way.

A few merging points guided me. Some connections had been planted decades ago. In early 2000, I was heading to the UK from Switzerland to improve my English. I chose Cambridge, as the university there published many English books. I made new friends and connected with a student from Sweden.

Then, in 2001, I started working as a buyer's assistant. One day, the team of employees headed to a work outing, which involved music and good food and ended up with some fun on the dance floor. During that trip, someone suggested that I do something with my dancing as he was impressed with how I moved to the music.

His comment led me to enroll at the music school in Lucerne, Switzerland, and initiated my artistic journey. I attended the music school for about six months. And because my thoughts of

Be Human, Be Happy, Be YOU!

pursuing dance hadn't left, I planned my next adventure.

Six months later, I decided to look into different dance school options in urban settings. The choices were London or New York City. Because I was interested in hip-hop and R&B at the time, I decided that NYC would be a better fit. I visited New York for a week to check out some studios. Prior to heading there, out of the blue, I decided to reach out to my friend from Sweden; we hadn't been in touch much. In a conversation, she told me that her sister's best friend was currently dancing in New York and shared her email address and phone number with me.

Back in the early 2000s, cell phones were far different than they are today. International plans were too costly. Therefore, I contacted her via email and we planned to meet at the studio at some point while I was in NYC.

During my trip, I stayed at the YMCA, where the rooms were so small I felt like I was in a cell. This forced me to be out and about. I spent most of my days walking around the city, exploring it, and connecting to the new vibe.

Flow of Life

One fun experience was when I walked down to Battery Park from Central Park. I desperately had to use the bathroom, so I went inside the National Museum of the American Indian, knowing there had to be a restroom.

After that break, I got hungry, so I decided to stop at a McDonald's around the corner. As I walked in, a woman stopped me and said: "Hi, how are you?" It sounded like she knew me, and she did. She was the security guard at the museum. We talked briefly and to her disappointment, I didn't visit the museum. She told me to come back as it is a magnificent museum. I haven't returned yet, but will make it there one day.

This brief interaction and many others reconfirmed why this was the city for me. I loved the openness of the people, the curiosity, and the willingness to get to know you, even if only for a brief moment. I couldn't wait to see how my meet-up with my new Swedish friend would go.

When we finally connected, we immediately hit it off. She took me along to hang out with her friends,

Be Human, Be Happy, Be YOU!

and we even attended some off-stage concerts with Coldplay at the Video Music Awards.

She showed me the city, which I was eager to learn more about. That week, I also met many interesting people—Rob Thomas from Matchbox 20 and Aretha Franklin—which added to knowing NYC was the place I wanted to be.

More incredible moments happened. My new friend was also moving out of her shared apartment that summer. Her roommates would have had to look for someone to take over her room. Thanks to this connection, I was able to take over her space and already had an apartment set up.

Retelling this story makes me realize how incredible certain moments become when we let them unfold in their own time without fear of getting hurt or lost. Even the story of how I met my husband that year has its own little crazy coincidences, which I will get into more in the next chapter.

Another more recent story of the flow of life is when I attended my second 10-day silent retreat. Actually, let me start with my first 10-day silent retreat, another story that has directed me to where I am today.

After I got married, it wasn't easy to find a job because of my lack of US-approved degrees. One of my first jobs was as a volunteer with Safe Horizon, an organization that helps people with various disputes through mediation. When the organization offered to pay to attend a course for mediation training at Columbia University, I enrolled. Once there, I met a woman, another student, who shared with me her troubles with emotions when I told her about my difficulty keeping my anger in check.

She told me about a meditation practice that helped her be more at ease and less reactive, which was something I wanted to get better at.

This meditation practice is called *Vipassana* and is one of India's most ancient techniques of meditation.

When you start out, this practice requires you to attend a 10-day silent retreat. You are not allowed to bring your phone, books, journal, or anything that would help deal with boredom and attempts to distract you, including exercising in any form.

Be Human, Be Happy, Be YOU!

Three months after I completed my yoga teacher training in February 2010, the woman's recommendation came to mind, and I was ready to explore this retreat. I had no expectations nor did I know what to expect. I remember my spouse dropping me off at 5 a.m. at the Port Authority, from where I took a 5-hour bus ride to Greenfield, MA, and then had to take a cab to the final destination.

Once the program started, we were not allowed to speak or interact with others. At that time, I was sharing a room with four other women, and we grew close to each other even though we couldn't exchange any words. The retreat was quite intense, especially because I had never meditated for longer periods of time before. We had to meditate six hours a day, at times without being able to move. It sounds like torture, and at least it felt that way. However, once you committed to the practice and understood the process, it got easier.

Interestingly, I didn't know until a few years ago that *Vipassana,* which means "to see things as they really are," can also be translated into "mindfulness." Seeing the connection today blows my mind.

Flow of Life

Some time ago, I asked the well-known mindfulness teacher, Jon Kabat-Zinn, what it takes to be a mindfulness teacher. He said to go on a 10-day silent retreat at least once a year. Wow, once a year? It's been about ten years, and I have only gone to one. I remember thinking, *I've got a long way to go.* At the time, my son was only six years old. When our son got older, I felt more comfortable and ready to pursue an annual 10-day retreat if my spouse was willing to take care of my household duties in the meantime.

And here is when my second 10-day retreat began. This past year, my spouse and I got into a discussion about gift-giving at the holidays. I remember heading to brush my teeth when this glorious idea came to my mind: I would love to be gifted one 10-day retreat per year.

He looked at me concerned and wondered, "You're sure that's what you want?"

Yes, it was, and it didn't take much time for me to look for the next available retreat. As these specific retreats are free, they fill up fast and open six months before they start. It was already November, and the next one I could attend was in June 2023. I signed up without hesitation even though it began on my spouse's birthday. He willingly let me register for the retreat.

As we got closer to the retreat date, it turned out that my son had a recital on the exact date of my spouse's birthday and that I didn't want to miss. I decided to change my attendance from being a student to being a server, which meant that I would be helping out in the kitchen and other things to facilitate a smooth experience of the retreat for the students.

There it was. A completely new experience, and what was also unexpected was that I would be ending the part-time job I had worked at for the past two years at the end of May. It was a new beginning, a new way to start my focus on mindfulness. Even though I would love to attend the retreat as a student again—I haven't done a full 10-day silent retreat in over 13 years—I accepted this change of events with an open heart.

What happened during this different experience summarizes the past few months and even years. I

Flow of Life

found myself with around twenty other servers. We were creating relationships with each other while serving the students, which wouldn't have been possible if we had been students, for students are not allowed to speak to one another. I can't describe how much I learned in these ten days about myself and how others affect me. Every person had a different impact on me and taught me different lessons, which I will share in the chapter "Lessons Learned."

The purpose of mentioning this flow of life is that over six months, many things have changed, and even if the main plan remained, the outcome and lessons aren't something I could have predicted.

Every time we allow life to unfold as it presents itself, we can be positively surprised. I have realized that trusting our decisions, journeys, and life's happenings is hard. By practicing the flow of life and being present with what comes up, I believe we are forging a positive path toward happiness and life as it is while making it the best experience.

We all have lived in a flow of life, though we might not have been as aware of it. The more we notice that when life becomes easy, we let go of expectations, we "go with the flow," and we allow the flow of life to impact us significantly.

My Love

Early in life, I started looking for THE person to live my life with—my soulmate. My yearning to be loved and be in a relationship was strong. I believed that being happy included a relationship. I am not sure where I got this from. Now I know to be "happy" means to love me first to fully cherish the person I am with. It was a longer path to find this out. In this chapter, I share how relationships help us learn more about ourselves and how creating space for each other is the key to success.

I had been in three long-term relationships of different religions, cultures, languages, tendencies, likings, and backgrounds in Switzerland before I met my spouse in 2003. Trying to figure out what and who my soulmate is required a sense of knowing myself.

"Being myself" is a journey on the way to growing into the human I am. There are lessons I learn through relationships and various human connections. Only once I crossed "The Pond" did I embark on a deeper journey of discovering myself without knowing where I was going or where this journey would take me.

Obviously, twenty years later, it's easier to see where my life is taking me, but back then, I never thought that I would meet my knight in shining armor in a little restaurant/bar in Chinatown in the middle of NYC called "Good World."

It was the drive at the end of the night from Manhattan all the way into Queens that lit the fire. When I shared with him in a conversation that my favorite car is a Porsche Carrera 4S in dark blue and a tan interior, he was impressed, mainly because he's a car guy and he knew what kind of car it was. Who knew that I would meet someone in the middle of NYC who understood my love of cars?

Even after he dropped me off, more coincidences connected us. Within a few days, I had already met his mother and visited his home—not realizing that we shared so many connecting points—Switzerland, languages, cars, driving, traveling, and adventures, to name but a few.

My Love

I don't know what it was, but something made me believe he was the person I would be spending my life with. It wasn't anything I knew or told myself then. The relationship was developing.

Even five and a half years later, the way our wedding ceremony turned out, we couldn't have planned it. At first, we just wanted to get a marriage license at the New York City Marriage Bureau. In a conversation with my spouse-to-be's relatives about getting married, they offered to connect us with a lawyer they knew who could officiate.

Originally, the exchange of vows was supposed to have taken place in his office, but an unplanned fire drill occurred and everyone in the building had to leave. Luckily, the lawyer's secretary brought all the paperwork, so our ceremony could take place outdoors in a public park.

Why am I sharing this with you? My story isn't about the beauty of being in a relationship and finding our soulmate. It's more about realizing that if we're not searching for something or someone, and we move along our path to finding ourselves and

Be Human, Be Happy, Be You!

staying aware and in open conversations, the right people and events will cross our path.

* * *

As we go through life, we often strive to achieve certain goals. Remember the beginning of this chapter? I discussed my search for my soulmate. Going through those previous relationships helped me understand my needs and wants better. Being with different people revealed to me what kind of person I wanted to be with.

One of my last relationships was with a guy who was not a good driver, at least not to my taste. After that, I swore the person I would marry had to be a great driver, better than me.

The search wasn't the lesson. The lesson was that the more I believed in myself and knew what I wanted while I explored the world, the more sense of who I wanted to become solidified.

While preparing to write this book, I created a general timeline with specific main dates. As I studied the timeline, I noticed that when certain moments happened, they were also reflected in the completion of our prefrontal cortex.[1]

My Love

For those unfamiliar with this term, this is the front part of our brain, which isn't fully developed until about our mid-twenties. That's when we are able to understand consequences and complex thought processes.

With this knowledge and the awareness of my journey up until this point, I realized that everything can happen at the right time if we don't have a deadline or specific moment in mind.

Reflecting on my now-twenty-year relationship—fourteen years of marriage, nine of those with a child (as of 2023)—I have learned that leading with love is what matters. There are many things we don't learn or can predict how they will play out in life. There isn't a playbook on how to live and love life. It is probably better that way. Here are a few reasons why living by experience and leading with love are key:

- We all have different experiences.
- Our perspectives are different.
- The evolution of our DNA influences us.

Be Human, Be Happy, Be You!

One way to connect our experiences and sense of being is through communication.

Communication has been the critical component to keeping the relationship with my spouse on affectionate terms. That certainly is not to say that our partnership is always rosy. There are challenges in keeping a household, preparing for a trip, and raising a child.

Communication is a vital tool to navigate and share our thoughts, not to keep them as they are but to allow them to be shared without judgment.

Communication is an effective tool and what I believe to be the foundation of a relationship. It also raises our sense of

- self-confidence,
- self-trust,
- self-love, and
- self-compassion.

When I compare my previous relationships with my current one, I can see how those four self-awareness aspects have improved my relationships. Time and

My Love

life experiences help us to understand ourselves better.

A relationship isn't the foundation for discovering a sense of self. Yes, a relationship can help us be more confident, trustworthy, loving, and compassionate. But it would be too much to ask of a partner to be responsible for my self-confidence, self-trust, self-love, and self-compassion, or to blame a partner for not providing those aspects.

In retrospect, I noticed that moving away from the comfort of my home in Switzerland, I had the opportunity to build strength within me, at least for the initial chunk. A sense of self was still growing at the beginning of our relationship, and interestingly enough, the motivation for building my confidence, trust, love, and compassion, was initially for the relationship.

Nevertheless, the focus was on me, not on my partner. I knew I had to make changes to myself to make this relationship work. That is not to say that the changes were only one-sided, for my spouse did his part as well.

Be Human, Be Happy, Be You!

Falling into an energy-sapping relationship can happen when it's all on you. Actually, I don't recall looking for any problems with my partner. I focused on myself and what I wanted—which was for this relationship to work no matter what. Luckily for me, we were in this together, and as far as I can tell, it has worked so far.

Many ways of how to show love and care for one another had to be relearned from growing up, especially knowing that we can love and be loved even if we aren't perfect. For example, I had misconceptions about ways in which my parents could share their love with me—through communication, support, and compassion.

As we grow up, we create our understanding of how we want to be loved by our parents. Most of the time, what we want and what our caregivers demonstrate don't always match. Depending on how aware we are about the love we are looking for, the ways we want to be loved will come up again in our relationships.

Building an awareness of our needs and wants with regard to love informs us about how we will

My Love

search for love. Challenges arise when we have a different perspective on how we want to be loved.

That's when communication comes in. Knowing the right vocabulary and words to share our thoughts, emotions, and experiences is still—and always will be—challenging. Despite the challenge, if we don't practice and share our thoughts no matter how imperfect and misunderstood they are, the less likely it is that we will have a successful relationship. I don't only mean a personal and private relationship with a spouse or partner, but also with friends, with associates at work, and many other places, as you will learn later in this book.

Being human is complex. I can't stress that enough. It makes it especially difficult when we want everything to flow easily and only wish to experience joyous moments. There's nothing wrong with wanting to feel and experience joy, though focusing only on positive moments, we would make our lives only half as exciting.

Just imagine if everything always went smoothly. If every day was predictable. If we knew how successful the day would be and how much we would accomplish? Where would the fun be? Not that I want stressful and frustrating things to happen. However, those unpleasant moments remind us what it means to be human. Those moments help us see the beauty of the more fortunate moments and those moments make us grow and evolve.

Here is an example from nature. Imagine where the world would be if we only had sunshine. We wouldn't be able to grow anything, and when it finally rained, as we already saw in California, the dried-out soil couldn't absorb the water and flooding occurred.

What happens if we don't allow little miscommunications and annoyances to reach the surface of our relationships? The relevant part is that we keep working on it. Once we become lazy about our relationship or not caring enough to bring up what rubbed us the wrong way, lo and behold, we are like the dried-up soil that can't deal with a deluge.

It is possible that we will experience even greater challenges than those occurring now. Our relationship needs to cope with them. We must keep communication open between the ebbs, flows, and

My Love

tedious parts of life. When we reinvent ourselves and our relationships, excitement and joy will stay for the long haul.

Another thing I have discovered is that we must bring honesty to our relationships. When daily life takes over, and our focus on making a relationship work falls into a morning routine, working all day, and ending the day with some non-communicative actions, we can quickly fall into a *Groundhog Day*—same stuff, different day. That's when our alarms should sound. These are the moments we want to handle with care. Those are moments of reinvention, recommunication of what we want in life, this moment, this relationship.

Daily life can quickly take over. If we don't practice awareness, we won't even notice how our life and relationships are slipping away beneath our feet. If you have children, you probably have noticed those moments when you look at them and they seem so grown up.

When we are in a loving relationship or friendship, we likely won't notice such moments as drastically. They will gradually adjust, and suddenly,

Be Human, Be Happy, Be You!

we feel like we're waking up from a dream or a nightmare and wonder, "How did we get here?"

In my opinion, this question comes up when we pay too much attention to a greater goal in mind—that house, that vacation, that car, that amount in our bank account. Not that there is anything wrong with that. What those things do is take our attention away from the beauty of the present moment. Noticing how the light shines on our partner's face or watching his/her/their eyes glance at us in an unexpected moment, like walking past one another.

Well, I am not going to romanticize relationships. Such moments aren't there all the time, though the more we practice, the clearer and more aware we are when they do arise. These do not occur when we search for them, but rather, when they are least expected.

Our daily stresses, responsibilities, and commitments take over our thoughts and life. And when we're honest with ourselves, we only have 24 hours a day and seven days a week, which we tend to fill to the rim, so there aren't even moments when we can relax and do nothing.

My Love

Does doing nothing sound boring? Maybe, though, when you are bored together, amazing things can happen. My spouse and I have such dull moments, and it still amuses me. Once we drove for four hours to purchase maple syrup and returned home the same day. Considering our love for driving and spending time in a car together, there couldn't have been any better place to be.

Okay, driving such a distance might not be the most environmentally friendly activity either, yet it provided a wonderful bonding experience. Traveling quite a distance just to buy some maple syrup is not something we do every day. The trip meant time spent together talking about the world and deepening our relationship.

What is something you and your partner bond over? Maybe food, dancing, biking, walking, swimming,—well, anything really. It's up to you both to figure out what lights you up.

When I look at how I relate to my relationship now versus back in 2003, the most remarkable difference is that I have grown more confident and trusting in myself. In the early days, I was looking for confirmation and acknowledgment of my relationship. That has changed for the better.

As mentioned earlier, our prefrontal cortex isn't developed until about our mid-twenties. I assume that we seek partners who give us what we were missing while we grew up and how we received love. What can happen is that we will rely on what the partner has to offer and underestimate what we bring to a relationship.

Most importantly, we don't change solely for other people but do so because we believe in the change.

One example that demonstrates the growth and trust in my relationship is that before we got married, I had some tendencies to get upset and take things personally all the time. I didn't know how to manage my frustration and anger well. I remember my spouse giving me an ultimatum that he would have to reconsider having a future together if I didn't change my behavior.

On a side note, when I mention this memory to my spouse, he doesn't remember saying it like that, so it might or might not be true; we will never know.

My Love

What I do know is that this conversation led me to the "Self-Help" section at Barnes & Noble.

I knew that he was the person I wanted to spend my life with. I knew that my outbursts weren't healthy and I knew I had to do something. I remember picking up the book *Why Good People Do Bad Things* by Debbie Ford. The title resonated with me because I knew I had to figure out why and what was fundamentally off. Thus started my journey of self-discovery.

I was not only changing for my spouse and his wishes, but ultimately, I was changing for my own benefit. Even though the initiation of this change was external, the change was necessary for me to become a better version of myself.

Changing my attitude and approach definitely didn't happen overnight. There were many times that I was reminded that I was still acting as I had in the past. Then I had to put my foot down and remind him that change takes time. It takes dedication, and until this day, twenty years into our relationship, I am still evolving into who I am. I want to become an inspiration in a relationship, not only with my spouse but also with my son and other people who cross my path.

The best part about the "ultimatum" for change is that I began reading more books than I ever had before. More importantly, it was the beginning of taking the mindfulness journey into my own hands and establishing a more profound sense of who I am.

Thank you, Life, for helping me meet my spouse in a restaurant/bar in NYC, for my parents allowing me to travel across the Atlantic Ocean, and for the immense curiosity that lies within all of us when we can let go of what we think we need to be happy.

Let life be the guide to take us on a marvelous journey—without pressure, stress, and expectations.

Endnote

[1] www.ncbi.nlm.nih.gov/books/NBK499919/

Me, My Child, & Mindfulness

Throughout the previous pages, I gave you a glimpse of how mindfulness knocked on my door in different ways. Already from a young age, I understood and decided that each of us is walking our own path. Only later on did I add the awareness that I did not and do not need to gain acceptance from others. No matter how much we share with others, no one will ever know more about what we need and want better than we do—even if we are not always consciously aware of those needs and wants.

People we meet and spend time with are only our mirrors. They don't hold a perception, expectations, hopes, and dreams for us; they express their own perceptions, hopes, and dreams for themselves. We could say that when we have children, that perception changes, but I am not so sure of that.

We have hopes and dreams that we—our children and us—will succeed in life, be happy, and be surrounded by good people, and at the same time, they are our hopes and dreams.

Be Human, Be Happy, Be YOU!

Our children can be the extension of our hopes and dreams. It isn't always easy to separate ourselves from them. Reflecting on being a parent is definitely another layer of exploring being ourselves, finding happiness, and recognizing our humanity.

The title of this book, *Be Human, Be Happy, Be You,* is an acknowledgment that the gift of mindfulness is in all of us. When we look at the eleven mindfulness attitudes, they all show up in our lives in one way or another. And all it takes is a reminder of how we can notice and add them to our lives and expand the gratitude of imperfections.

You might have noticed that most of the stories in the book are from my own perspective. Even though in this particular chapter, my spouse plays a role in raising our son. I can only speak for my experiences and how I felt going through them. That doesn't mean that we as a couple weren't discussing or looking for solutions together through those experiences. I am sharing what I have witnessed and explored.

Becoming a mother played a significant role in establishing the foundation of my focus and dedication to the practice of mindfulness and the deep longing to bring this beautiful teaching to you.

Our son was almost two years old when I lost my job of six years as a purchasing agent for a German firm. I found myself in a situation I had never been in before. Being let go from a job in which I loved my co-workers like family, being given reasons of my termination I couldn't follow, and thinking that the decision was unfair and inconsiderate, I was upset and resentful towards my "then" boss. Talking and reflecting on my disbelief with people close to me, I was reminded of my interest in returning to school.

Coming from Switzerland and having difficulty finding a job, let alone getting an interview with my credentials, I took this opportunity to make up for something I yearned to achieve. I declined the offer to stay at work for another two months and immediately applied to the community college nearby.

As it all played out, I was accepted within a few weeks. I found myself yet in another unique situation—going to college in the States. It was exciting to take classes I was interested in. I discovered my interest in writing, something I had struggled with in Switzerland. I took art classes, anatomy, communication, and anthropology. The college offered a wide assortment of classes that ultimately guided me toward mindfulness. The opportunities at the college sparked a new interest in learning that I never had growing up. Through this experience, I discovered my true life interests in people, friendships, and endless conversations about life.

Along this journey of studying, meeting deadlines, and learning new crafts, I was also a mother of a toddler. In his first two years, I provided a safe and healthy environment to let him grow and become stronger. I enjoyed this time very much; it was nurturing. And as he grew older, he became more of his own being, expressing his needs and wants, sharing strong thoughts and resistance towards what we needed to do, the challenges of being a mother increased.

I started to notice my limitations and expectations of him. A new space was created: me, him, and *our* space. Understanding what it was that I "want," what it was that he "wants," and where we could meet in the middle has been a constant struggle. Giving and receiving. Responding and reacting. Inquiring and demanding. It was a battle. There were days I wondered how people could become parents. How is it possible to raise a child? What does it take?

I kept seeing my own challenges growing up. My parents faced challenges when I was little and as I grew into my being. I now understand why my mother wished me to have a child of my own. And while that wish was valuable, I also recognize that this learning from my parents' challenges provided a huge opportunity to create a relationship with my son that I didn't realize was what I was looking for.

There are many "non-proud mom" moments, which could be expected of a new mother. I had to take a deep look at myself, my challenges, and my expectations. I was pulled into the "should" of being on time and following societal expectations while disconnecting from my child.

It took years for me to improve my communication with and understanding of myself and my child, and I am still learning. My mindfulness practice supports me in not judging myself, not putting blame and shame on myself. It was my practice that encouraged me to keep moving toward my family and to keep bringing curiosity and kindness into the mix.

Taking care of another human being can become extremely difficult when we don't spend enough time caring for ourselves. During the first few years of being a mom, I learned that we never know what will happen as our offspring become their own beings.

The only thing I was and am able to do is to stay present. Let past experiences and future expectations take a back seat. They are helpful and important, yet they can change how we connect to ourselves and our child at this moment.

Life becomes even more complex when we throw a spouse and more children into the mix. One of the main reasons I decided to have a child was not because I had always wanted children, but rather, I wanted something that united my spouse and me.

What I did know is that if I had children, I always wanted to have two. When I found myself in tumultuous situations and observing friends expecting their second child, I couldn't imagine how I would do the same. My challenge was giving myself the time I needed to reflect on who I was becoming, ensuring that I was raising my child to reach his best opportunities, and giving him the connection and stability of parenthood. These considerations led me to make a firm decision to give my full attention to my son without adding more siblings to the mix. My hope was to not put pressure or expectations on him that I would regret.

Choosing not to have more children was definitely a decision with many consequences. Telling you this story only demonstrates that we need to make hard choices in our lives. When we make them with awareness and deep consciousness, we won't regret our decision, even if that means not knowing if the decision would have been just fine or if it was the right choice after all.

I was reminded of my decision when my brother announced that he and his wife were expecting their second child. I was drawn back into a loop of questioning, "Why couldn't I do it?" "Why couldn't I get my stuff together and provide my son with a sibling?"

Be Human, Be Happy, Be YOU!

It took me a few moments to revisit my past decision and looking into my reasoning. I looked back on how I felt when my son was two or three years old and remember being compassionate, understanding, and patient. I also reflected on times that were challenging and recognized my limitations. My relationship with my son, the opportunities we have as a family, no matter the circumstances and decisions, the key component for me is that we are fully ourselves, without pressure or stress.

The decisions I make come from a conscious place. If we are lucky, more choices can be revisited and changed, and some, like this, can't. Instead of dwelling on made decisions, I remind myself why I chose them in the first place.

Reflecting on our decisions allows every one of us to make choices we stand behind. Sometimes this means accepting what it is by letting go and letting be and finding a beginner's mind to move forward.

While this journey of being a parent is only the beginning, we keep learning many lessons. One of the most important ones is how we do our best to

Me, My Child, & Mindfulness

return to the present moment. Connecting to our senses is a way that is always accessible. We can see, feel, touch, hear, taste, and connect to what is. When we do this without judgment, without striving to be something, or getting something in particular, we have no choice but to be present and make a connection with our children. One of the best-fitting mindfulness attitudes that creates a meaningful relationship with our children and the decisions we make is humor.

Being present is a foundation we build on in a long-lasting relationship, and it might not start with our child. I am curious to see what parenthood still has to offer and what struggles we will face. And without looking too much into the future, I remind myself that the gift is in the present. I cherish the moments when my son calls from the other room and says: "Mom, I love you."

Being a parent has helped me tremendously in understanding how to get hold of my own stories, how I was raised, and what impacts my upbringing had on me. I am constantly figuring out what messages and teachings I want to continue and which my brother and I lived as truthfully as possible. Even though there were behaviors and disciplines she wanted us to follow, there was always enough room to be ourselves and explore our emotions. I see that my mother encouraged me to find myself and never let her opinion limit me, even if that wasn't always possible.

As I explore and share my experiences and learnings through Mindful Being, I feel my urge to provide you with a sense of self and encourage you to live each moment as who you are.

My mother was—and still is—the catalyst of being an "artist of life," another way to interpret mindfulness. Living like an artist means figuring out a way to move with your environment while staying true to who you are. At my current age of 44, there were only a few moments in which when I had to "be someone else," though I don't remember those well. Most of the time, I found my way, and I could express myself with all my emotions wherever I was, even if not everyone liked them or could deal with them. Of course, I had to learn not to overdo it.

Me, My Child, & Mindfulness

Expressing our emotions freely helps us to have a healthier inside. There is less built-up tension in our nervous system and other parts of our bodies. Our brain allows more creativity when life gets tough and we are less resistant to new ideas and possibilities.

Growing up, I told myself that I wanted to raise my child exactly like my parents had raised me. By leading with that mindset, I allowed myself to be like them, and once I was there, I could decide what worked and what didn't. It's almost impossible not to carry forward at least some of the traits and characteristics of our caregivers. It would be strange if we didn't. We lived with them for an extended period and also in a time when we learned what it meant to be human. Additionally, we also carry forward the traits of our ancestors and those have a vast influence on us as well.

I am raising my son similar to the way my mother raised me, as well as adding more layers. As we move through life and gain awareness of what we missed or had too much of growing up, we adjust our behaviors and how we treat others. In my case, I wanted more love from my parents—the love shown with hugs, kisses, and encouragement.

While I'm sure I received that kind of love, why do I still feel I missed them? Maybe because there was more judgment and discipline, or was that more my perception? Observing my childhood from a distance and thinking more deeply, I had it all. Most of all, I was given a great sense of safety and security at home. Even if my personal take was slightly different, all my hopes and dreams were of existence, just not when and how I wanted the love. Hmm, does this sound familiar?

My son is doing the same when he says, "You are mean," or "You don't care." I guess that is the dysregulated self in us, something internally that wasn't sitting well with the external experience at that given moment.

As I write this, I am learning a lot about our personal experiences and the experience of others, in this case, my son's. Over the past nine years of being with my son, I have discovered that we do the best we can and know to this point. My belief that giving him what he wants when he wants it is not what we

Me, My Child, & Mindfulness

are here to do. Raising a child requires a healthy dose of awareness. Is what I provide my child based on my perception of what I was missing? Is it because I saw somewhere that it's working, or am I aware and conscious about this? What do I really want to teach my child?

This book is not about how to raise a child. This book is solely about raising awareness of our thoughts, actions, and decisions for ourselves and the people around us. Questioning our behaviors and giving them attention to see what drives us to make those choices is based on

- Our past experiences
- A goal-oriented outcome, and
- An inner belief that this is the right choice.

I also remind myself that nothing is written in stone and can be changed. That's where the practice of letting go/letting be comes in. Even though we don't want our children to be at the mercy of our perhaps mistaken decisions, sometimes that's the only way we learn.

Be Human, Be Happy, Be YOU!

For me, the most important lesson as a parent was to learn how to apologize sincerely and acknowledge my mistakes. Mistakes also mean that some decisions work better in one situation and less in others. Instead of beating us down for not providing the right experience, feedback, or direction, there may be something we can take away and learn from our missteps.

I saw a beautiful video[1] the other day in which a teacher wrote ten equations on the board; the last one needed to be corrected. The students started laughing and making jokes about the silly mistake the teacher had made. Little did they know that this was the lesson the teacher was teaching them about making mistakes in life. He pointed out that it is so much easier to be judged and demonstrate the faults than to find the good and the accomplishments we made.

When we practice giving more compliments and seeing the good in people, we will not only help our children and anyone we meet with a positive experience, we also teach ourselves to see the accomplishments and good we do.

Me, My Child, & Mindfulness

This brings me to a topic I will discuss in a later chapter—the importance of "Unconditional Love" for ourselves. The more we practice unconditional love for ourselves, the easier it is for our children to take on this mindset and way of living. We can show them that mistakes will happen. However, that's not how we measure ourselves; it's to learn from them and make life better for ourselves and others.

Only recently have I slowly gotten the hang of what it means to be a parent. It will take my whole life to grasp and put into full action, though at least I understand the foundation. We are here to guide our children, give them a safe home, and provide direction on how to be great human beings. While we guide them, we must also face inward to see what tendencies are still ingrained in us and what patterns we can shift into a more open and inviting environment.

We all have heard before that our children won't remember what we say but how we make them feel. So, our actions speak louder than words, and it's up to us to make this connection with our children. Even when we worry, get stressed out, and have thoughts of uncertainty about our children's future, we want them to feel and be safe.

We can't foresee the future; we don't know what jobs they will have and what will be needed ten or twenty years from now. What we do know is that they are in our care right now. Depending on their age, they want our full attention and involvement in what they do and, at the same time, want to figure out life for themselves.

As parents and caregivers, we are learning with them, and our training will be in how we meet them where they are without imposing our worries and struggles onto them. They may have it figured out in their way, and by collaborating and exchanging our experiences, no matter how different they are, we learn to live *with* them instead of *for* them. They might thank us later, even without the acknowledgment we anticipated and hoped for.

It's incredible how quickly our kids grow up. I can't stop time, and I want my child to explore the world on his own time and let him be a child, while supporting him in whatever he wants to pursue. It's tough to say how my methods of upbringing will affect my son in the future. One thing is for sure—it will have an impact on him—hopefully, a positive one. Yet that is out of my control.

What I can control is how I speak and act in front of him, which isn't always praise-worthy. In those situations, our son lets me know that my ways of speaking and acting are far from perfect. What I will say now might not be approved parenting advice, though I have come to the conclusion that occasionally debating with my spouse in front of our son I believe to be healthy. I want my child to learn from his parents—who love him—that disagreeing is human. I want my son to know that the discussion is not about the disagreement; it's about how we resolve problems and still love each other. I see it as another way of demonstrating "Unconditional Love."

As I write this, I am learning more about my intentions of being a parent. I see it as an experiment. From the moment I first discovered that I was pregnant until the end of my being, I never know where my actions and non-actions will lead. I will see the outcome in my son's actions, and he'll teach me

Be Human, Be Happy, Be YOU!

how to be a better person.

Being a parent is learning what it means to be human and seeing things in myself and my spouse in ways I would never know about or discover. It adds another layer to experiencing life through a child's eyes. I don't think I would've learned as much about myself and mindfulness had I not embarked on this parenting journey.

Followed by my own experience as a parent, I now move into the discoveries I made through recently losing my father, reflect on my relationship with him, and what I've learned along the way.

Endnote

[1] "Teacher Makes Shocking Error But His Response is Priceless," youtube.com/watch?v=xq2d2i948sI&t=2s

Living and Dying

When my dad passed away on October 17th, 2022, so many questions and wishes remained unanswered. We will never have the opportunity of experiencing another verbal exchange. Now, all I have is what I have. In the following pages, I will share more details on his passing, our relationship, and how even in such moments, staying in the flow of life can play a significant role.

While I reflect on his passing, I am given the chance to discover many new insights into how we can live life to the fullest without regret and missed opportunities. I realized that the previous four years of dedicating and guiding in the practice of mindfulness prepared me for this moment.

For most of my life, I have been looking for recognition of what I have done and achieved. The time of reflection provided another perspective on how to embody our humanness and find happiness in being ourselves despite what people think, say, and do.

Be Human, Be Happy, Be YOU!

A few years ago, I was upset that my family didn't ask me about my practice and mindfulness teachings, thinking that if they didn't inquire, they didn't care. Once I truly considered and welcomed their non-engagement, I understood that one doesn't exclude the other. I know now that they had other worries; they didn't know what to ask or be interested in, and my activities were not as tangible as working as a purchasing agent or administrative assistant in a firm. That realization wasn't easy to swallow, though it meant that I would not be resentful or hurt by my unmet expectations.

Over the past two years, I took the opportunity to tell my parents how much they mean to me and how much I appreciate all their actions and support. Instead of waiting for what I expected them to say and do, I explained to them my takeaways from having them as my parents.

The conclusion of my actions was that there were no regrets. I had taken my destiny into my own hands. It wasn't up to them to have me recognized. Instead, it was up to me to live my greatest life.

Living and Dying

Otherwise, there would always be a missing piece that no one else could give me.

Approaching my parents this way allowed me to let them hear about their efforts, investment, and received love. I don't know how my revelation affected them, as we weren't a family of many words, especially regarding emotional experiences. That said, I was able to choose my own ending to this chapter with my father by offering my parents unconditional love.

Another excellent lesson for me was comprehending that love isn't always—probably more often than not—shared in ways we would like to see and feel it. As we move through life, we have a certain idea of how we want to be loved. For some, it's holding each other's hands, hugging, saying "I love you"; for others, it's checking in daily, saying kind words, letting us make our own decisions, providing support, or all of the above.

When how we want to be loved isn't happening, we may believe others don't love us. I rediscovered that wasn't true. In my experience, I learned that based on the way my parents were raised with high expectations, no sense of felt love, and minimum communication, they couldn't show me love in the way I envisioned it.

Looking back at the love my dad shared with me, I can now see how his actions and words affected me. My father and I share some inspiring personalities that I now feel more connected to—the energetic, entrepreneurial, organized, possibility-oriented, and heartfelt way of living.

Sometimes love is expressed through material things that don't necessarily reflect our expectations or the emotions we understand. Even though receiving gifts might not be what we want, the person expressing love in that way might not know a different "love" language. When we accept the material things, we might be able to feel it as an "I love you." We want to learn how to look past the material things and see what the actions are telling us.

What I do see now is how my dad truly cared for his well-being. As much as he wasn't able to have difficult conversations about relationships, he demonstrated that we need to find things in our lives

Living and Dying

that make us truly happy. There are no conditions for that. It's our job to ensure we as individuals are happy from within. Even if I sometimes thought he wasn't completely happy, that portrayal was solely my reflection. Not his. And even if it was, it wasn't up to me to decide.

Unfortunately, he never shared many of his personal experiences, his inner struggles. Who can blame him for that? Who wants to openly share what's going on within? Being vulnerable is not an easy thing to tackle, and as much as I'd love to have had these conversations with him to get to know him better and build a deeper understanding of who he was and his most significant challenges, those questions will remain unanswered.

Over the course of our lives together, I learned a great deal from my father. I learned that we must decide what works for us and lead by example. The lack of communication and difficult exchanges with him disconnected us from having a deeper relationship. At the same time, our interactions taught me that we all are on our own journeys. No one will ever completely understand us. No one will walk in our shoes. No one will be able to remove our pain. We have to do the work on our own.

That might sound like a lonely path, though if we all take care of our own internal struggles, we can then get together with more ease and compassion. Looking back at specific conversations and conflicts, I realize my parents couldn't comfort my needs, pains, and feelings of neglect.

Seeing my upbringing from that angle makes me comprehend how limiting we can be as humans. We need help incorporating our own views and those of others. It's challenging to give our perspective and the opposing side's attention in a balanced way. We end up focusing on our perspectives and how we see the world, not grasping that we automatically disregard what the other person is going through, instead of integrating both sides.

The challenge in considering two sides is that it takes time, and most importantly, it takes two. Both parties have to be willing to step outside themselves and out of their comfort zone to understand the issue at hand.

What is the point of bringing these issues up in the first place, and what is the greater good in getting

Living and Dying

the struggles resolved? Both parties need to see the same outcome. Otherwise, the discussion and resolution won't happen as the parties will steer in different directions. Instead of resolving the issue, a deeper well is dug and the parties drift apart.

Before people even begin to discuss the core issues, they have to be absolutely clear on the outcome being sought. This means first having to work through the challenges by ourselves and understanding what the bigger picture is.

You may wonder, "Why is this important? Why would I even want to go that far?"

For me, the answers are simple. Anything else would only be talk and no action. Our conversations remain superficial and we will never actually find the core issue.

If we don't go deeper to get to the root, we will continuously encounter the same problem again and again, especially when dealing with the people who will be part of our lives for a while, like parents, partners, children, friends, and even supervisors and coworkers.

Be Human, Be Happy, Be YOU!

Traveling across the ocean and growing a family and building a foundation in another country wasn't a deliberate choice at first. As I shared in "My Love," life and love brought me here. From this viewpoint, I can now see the reason. More than a decade has passed since I settled down in the States in 2009. Over time, I discovered that I had moved across the ocean to build a healthier relationship with my family in Switzerland.

I admit that I can be very overwhelming at times, especially when it comes to conflict. I come from a good place, though recently, my dear brother shared with me that I can be intimidating. That wasn't the first time I heard that. I don't shy away from difficult conversations, and sometimes my emotions and how I express them come across harsh and unfiltered.

Resistance to talk about challenging topics bothers me the most. I used to be unaware of how the other party struggled with my sharing where I was coming from. There have been numerous situations about how I showed up, how the topic made the other person feel, and what state of mind they were in that day.

Living and Dying

I've learned a lot in my marriage and with my child: our love isn't compromised by our challenges but strengthened. I have discovered that being away from my family provided me with the opportunity to see them from a distance, which gives my family more space with my energetic and sensitive way of moving through discussions. The distance helped us see each other for who we are and what we do for each other. It didn't avoid debates, though it limited our discussions to the important ones. The distance helped us be with each other in a more understanding way, at least from what I can tell. It gave me more space not to be entangled in the little things and to start appreciating the more important parts of life.

What if we are unable to come together and resolve the debate mutually? How do we come to terms with a situation when the other person isn't willing? The last disagreement I had with my father that didn't feel good was a situation that had happened similarly in the past. This was the first time I chose a different path. We were driving home from my dad's chemo treatment. A new car seat for my nephew was in the back seat and had not been secured properly. I tried to fix it but couldn't make it work.

When we arrived home, my dad wanted to take a look and fix it. The way I responded to his efforts was to not even try because I had already looked. I kept talking and tried to keep him away from working on the car seat. He harshly commented that I was talking too much, a complaint I recall for as long as I can remember. (If you know me, you know how true that is.) Nevertheless, I was hurt by his comment.

That moment was the first time I didn't respond. I sat down, let the comment and my emotions settle, and figured out a way to move past the situation. Subconsciously, I used some of the "11 Attitudes of Mindfulness" and focused on the following three: acceptance, letting go and letting be, and a beginner's mind.

All eleven could be a great fit. And here is why I picked those three. First, when we are face to face with someone we care about and can't get on the same page about an issue or situation, those three attitudes can help us get back on the right track.

We can start with "acceptance." Acceptance doesn't mean I condone your actions. Rather, it can sound like, "I see you, I hear you, and I don't agree with you." In that moment, I accepted what he said and that I was hurt. When we begin there, it allows us to see with a new set of eyes, and by adding "letting go and letting be," we acknowledge the action and non-action of the other and move on. We don't let the cause of disruption determine our next steps. Letting go and letting be go hand in hand with acceptance.

This is not to say that what the other person did is okay or that we don't care. Practicing mindfulness means we accept the situation, are present, and that we are at peace with the statement or action even if we disagree.

This can be very difficult, especially when we see the other person is in the wrong, whether it be disrespect, hurt, or any other painful actions toward us. We must come to terms with the ache we go through on our own. We can't make someone else take care of our emotions and the way we feel, or be responsible for them.

There are moments when a judgmental statement from a person we love hurts us more than from others, even if the words used are the same. That does not mean condoning the statement, but to accept it. At the same time, mindfulness teaches us to let the hurt go so that we can move into a new experience with the person.

By using "a beginner's mind," we can establish a new relationship. We must reestablish a new foundation and boundaries that let us move forward in a way that makes us grow, learn, and build stronger and lasting relationships in the long run.

In the example with my father and the car seat, it didn't feel right to bring my realization that the exchange had hurt my feelings and discuss a resolution. This was a situation I had to accept and begin again on my own. Still, I wished we would have been able to build a deeper communicative connection. And at the same time, when we find a more fitting connection to one another that leaves behind

Living and Dying

what happened and focuses on a new relationship with the current situation, we inform each other that our care and love are way more important than being right.

I am happy to say that over the years, we were able to form a solid father-daughter relationship that defined what it meant to learn from each other. The greatest lessons learned were to accept each other for who we are, to let go and let be of the things that hurt us, and build a beginner's mind around the relationship we did have.

As I am reminded of all the teachings my father gave me, all the experiences I took away, and the beautiful unspoken gestures he provided, will be noticed and cherished for as long as I remember.

We can't always choose what we wish to remember. Everyone has the right to live a life they desire, which often doesn't match reality. Instead of focusing on how we want others to show up for us and how we think they could benefit from taking advantage of our way of living, we can open up and see how other people's ways of doing things could improve our lives and bring our way of living to them. All we know is what we know; others will likely never see life through our lenses.

Witnessing my dad's life, I've come to understand the statement, "Life is too short." We don't know what illnesses, challenges, and pains will cross our lives.

What has helped me appreciate and be grateful for life is by being present and aware. Yes, taking trips, eating delicious meals, and spending quality time away with loved ones are great; we can't just bank on those kinds of experiences all the time. We can see the magnificence right here when we see the beauty in the now and how every unpleasant experience is connected to a pleasant experience. The smaller the moments you collect, the greater the memory will remain.

What I am absorbing from my dad's relatively short life (he was two months short of 69) is that there is so much more we don't know than what we do know. It also came clear in my father's last few moments of life and how we, as a family, faced his passing. We recognized that life happens how it happens. That is not to say that we can lean back and

Living and Dying

do nothing. We must act. We must speak up. We must live the life we feel called to live, and life will happen with us.

Even my father's last few months were so timely. The last time the whole family—my mother, my brother, his wife, and their son, as well as my spouse and our son—came together was the night before our departure to New York in August. My dad gathered all his energy to make it to dinner, even though his body was at a breaking point. He must have known this would be his last time with all of us together.

My dad, my mom, and I had many conversations leading up to the dinner about what we thought he could do or couldn't do. He decided for himself. The following day, after our departure back to the States, he ended up in the hospital and we all thought it might be the end. Though it wasn't. He pushed himself through.

Two months later, minus two days, he headed to the hospital in an emergency. I just returned from Los Angeles from a week at a conference. For some reason, I had to call my parents before I even walked into the house, and caught them on the way to the hospital. Catching up with my mom a few hours later, she informed me that he wasn't in good shape.

She was alone, as my brother had just left for his well-deserved trip before the second baby came, and they couldn't return home so quickly. And even though I just taken a domestic flight from LA, I decided to take the next plane that night to Switzerland to be with my mom and dad.

It was the last time I was able to be with them both together. My father's demise happened so fast, even though we knew this moment would come. Exactly two months after his last urgent visit to the hospital, it was time to say goodbye.

You are never prepared for such a loss. What's the meaning of living and dying? A beginning and an end. When we look at our lives closely, we start seeing that our lives are not finite. Even though our physical form might not be here, the memories, experiences, and the constant reminder of their being will remain.

Our lives are a continuation of a more incredible experience. What we attend to in our lifetime might

Living and Dying

be limited, yet something beyond our understanding and awareness had already happened before we were born on this planet.

We continued the journey, and once our physical life ended, that purpose and experience we were part of would find another path to continue in a form we don't know anything about.

My dad carried over the sense of business from his dad in a new way, and now it's our turn to move on in our own way.

When we realize how life is being continued through others, life becomes more interesting. We might find a way not to take life so seriously and discover that there is also a lot of joy in how we experience life. The more we pay attention and practice awareness, the less we get overwhelmed with getting life, decisions, and relationships right and wanting more genuine relationships, we start enjoying what we already have in the way it exists.

I wish there had been more experiences I could have shared with my dad. I remind myself that he's always here, even if not in human form. I see him in me, my son, my brother, and his sons, and when I

Be Human, Be Happy, Be YOU!

look at a flawless sunset. And then I remember life is flawless.

We are perfect, and our life experiences are perfect. It all depends on how we define perfection.

This aspect of expectations caused me much pain, living a perfect life of happiness on Christmas Eve and never discussing any "heartship" (hardship). I hope more people will discover that perfection is not when everything works out the way we anticipate. Perfection is when things work out better than what we could have imagined.

Lessons Learned

The lessons we learn give us the most insight into how we adjust our lives. In those lessons, we discover the humanness in all of us. There isn't a right or wrong. It's both. There isn't a you or me. It's both. And the more we can practice this, the more we can see how all experiences are welcome. The sooner we live our best life by being ourselves and being happy, the sooner we can make impactful connections. In this chapter, I will describe some situations that left me with life lessons. We never know where our challenges will lead us.

The first lesson I would like to share with you that had an immense impact on my self-value and reframing my experiences was in education. School was challenging for me. I loved going to school because of my classmates—the people around me, not the subject matter. It was a struggle to get decent grades. When we had to take a standard test determining if we were to go to the upper, middle, or lower class level, I ended up in the lower class. I was devastated. I remember crying in class because I compared myself to those who ended up in my class and didn't think I was doing as poorly. I saw myself as a failure, not good enough. At that time, I didn't realize that my parents felt my pain and did anything they could to give me a better experience.

Six months later, I was able to take another test and was able to move up to the next grade, though little did I know that being permitted to move up was due to a collaboration between my parents and the teacher. It wasn't because I was able to pass the test. When I found this out decades later, I couldn't believe it. I was relieved and confused simultaneously, not realizing that I hadn't been cutting it educationally, and yet something allowed it to happen. Maybe it was good; I didn't know my parents and teacher had influenced the decision.

Fast-forward twenty-one years. After I lost my job in 2016, I returned to school here in the States, not expecting much but hoping to get a US degree as I wanted a better chance of finding a job than six years prior.

Lessons Learned

Back at school, I had the opportunity to rediscover the joy of learning. It may be because I was in my mid-thirties when I returned or because I better understood what I liked and disliked. Either way, I started to love reading, writing, and learning things I never thought I could do, such as drawing, writing decent essays, and even math.

Trust me—school didn't come easy. I just used all the resources available, from going to the Student Center at the Westchester Community College to review every paper I wrote, visiting the library to find the books I needed, and practicing my drawings. I also deepened my interest in anatomy, physiology, and communication. These subjects filled me up; I was excited about enjoying school again while doing well.

A year later, I transferred to Purchase College to get a bachelor's degree in the arts and ended up excelling and trusting in my knowledge capacity. My successes fueled me to realize that the sky is the limit.

Once I completed this degree, I remember sitting with a friend at lunch, crying, not knowing what I was supposed to do with the degree. I became aware that much focus is put on attaining the diploma and demonstrate the accomplishments and hard work put into school to receive a degree, and then what?

Some of you might have already had a plan and something lined up to do. I can also imagine that more than a handful of you felt like me—uncertain about what happens next. It's not like a degree provides us with our next job and adventure on our life path. What it does give us is new opportunities.

While I was in college, I used the two-and-a-half years to guide me to my interests. I reflected on all the subjects I took and what intrigued me the most.

I realized that my interest in art, people, anatomy, communication, and even history (a subject I wouldn't say I liked growing up) had grown on me. In my last semester, I was a learning assistant in a psychology class. This opportunity allowed me to teach mindfulness to a room of fifty students only because I voiced being interested in teaching it. Everything fell into place. It was an experience I couldn't even imagine.

Lessons Learned

I continued exploring and wondering about what fit best with the genres and abilities I took classes in. I didn't know where to begin or where these topics would lead me. During my exploration, a friend invited me to a mindfulness event at a nearby elementary school because we had been discussing this topic extensively on our way to work in the city. That led to where I am today.

After attending that event, I talked with the presenter and asked how to pursue this mindfulness journey. Following her lead, I started taking classes for six months, building my knowledge.

Very often, we don't know where our connections will take us, who we will meet, and what opportunities we might encounter.

Even though I didn't use my degree to apply for a job and to continue my journey in the corporate world where I had left off, I discovered where I wanted to spend my life and work in.

Moving to the States exposed me to different norms of education, and attending college at a later stage in life required me to study and approach additional education in a way I would never have

Be Human, Be Happy, Be YOU!

chosen voluntarily. In my mid-twenties, I was over school; school and studying weren't my passion. Never in a million years would I have guessed I would be returning to school to get a bachelor's degree.

Nevertheless, that was one of the best choices I could have made for myself after moving here. Not only did it amp up my self-esteem in learning and school, it also allowed me to find my passion for people in a way I could have never imagined. Here it is again, "never imagined."

Life holds so many things we cannot even imagine. That's the beauty of life. Life offers opportunities that surprise and amaze us. Once I realized that I'd been building a foundation of all my interests, abilities, and everything I learned throughout my life, it all merged into focus.

* * *

The next lesson I learned was during my two-year mindfulness meditation teacher training. Thanks to this program and especially my mentorship group, I discovered a refined version of myself.

Lessons Learned

During the first year of training, my peer group pushed and challenged me in ways I can only remember from my childhood, figuring my way out in becoming an adolescent, followed by becoming an adult. The training was a rude awakening and yet a necessary one.

Some challenges included lingering grief from losing a peer who decided to leave the group early on and miscommunication on schedules. There were meetings after which I left depleted, exhausted, lonely, and unacknowledged. The unsaid words, the gestures, and the non-communication that followed tore me apart. It would sometimes take days to recover. I was in despair, questioning what mindfulness is. Why was I in this program? Is this what it's supposed to be like? I was halfway into the program. I still had eleven months to go. I had to choose:

1. Leave and follow the path one of our peers had already taken, or
2. Stay and find a way to deal with it.

Be Human, Be Happy, Be YOU!

I remember telling myself that I was in a mindfulness training. This can't be it. I should be able to figure this out. So, I chose to keep showing up. I kept reinventing myself by figuring out how to make a difference in my presence in the group.

I had a sticky note that said: "What can we do now? How can we move forward from here?" It was intended to be mentioned when we were stuck in our peer group. Funny enough, I never had to use it.

I felt left alone in a program of mentors, peers, teachers, and administrators and didn't know who else to turn to within the program.

Fortunately, during the pandemic, I built relationships that included people who moved and lived life to the fullest, like me. People who were emotionally available and who were able to listen to my experiences without judgment, without changing my environment, and helping me figure things out on my own while reminding me that I did my best, did what I could, and that there is nothing wrong with me.

Being a person who likes to work things out, I was at a dead end. Through a conversation with the

Lessons Learned

administrators and directors of the training, I learned about the program's background and discovered that a corporation was still behind it all, which to me meant it didn't have space for emotional challenges and exploration.

As much as we can learn a craft from renowned and talented teachers, there is only so much space for personal experiences. People in the administration might not have all the answers and resources to make it an environment where all wishes and needs can be considered. So, I started looking at it as a business and accepted that I wouldn't find everything I needed and was looking for in the program. I had to reframe my expectations of having my emotional experiences be met and cared for.

I stayed in the course with this new awareness without becoming cold and disconnected. Whenever we discussed group experiences and how to hold space when challenges came up, I shared my personal experience to let my peers know that there were still some unresolved issues in a kind and non-reactive way—focusing on impact rather than intent, being supportive rather than defensive.

Be Human, Be Happy, Be YOU!

Finally, the day came when one of my peers reached out and finally had the conversation I had longed for the past four months. I cannot describe to you what I experienced during that conversation. It was mindfulness at its finest. I felt relief, joy, hope, reassurance, and clarity. There was love, care, openness, acceptance, and, most significantly: acknowledgment.

Reflecting on my experience before, during, and after this meaningful conversation, I discovered that I had had this pain before. It became apparent to me that struggles and difficulties were right in front of me, especially moments with my parents in which I wanted to address the "elephant in the room"—our conflicts. All I got was resistance and questions about why we needed to discuss disagreements. They didn't see the purpose of discussing conflicts any further. I felt like an outcast in my own family because I was the only one who dared to bring up uncomfortable topics.

Lessons Learned

What transpired were a few realizations:

1. It's not always up to me to set the timeline for when to resolve an issue. It's about giving space to myself and the other people.
2. We all have many challenges that are not always visible in our lives. Sometimes we need more time to prepare to share what we are going through. Just because I am willing to open up and am ready to settle things doesn't mean everyone is.

These realizations led me to another great lesson learned during my two-year teacher training—how differently we each experience life. First, we must recognize that we are all unique and different. No one on this planet is identical. Even twins, triplets, or quadruplets are not precisely the same.

* * *

Be Human, Be Happy, Be YOU!

As part of our mindfulness training, we also learned about diversity, equity, inclusivity, and accessibility (DEIA). Experiencing tragic scenes of racial inequity and socio-economic differences, especially in the United States, was part of our program to learn more about how implicit bias, stereotypes, and racial framing subconsciously occur in our immediate environment.

I won't go into the details of what we learned, for that would exceed the scope of this book. What I can share is how these issues relate to my experience growing up and my personal challenges. I am sure you will find some points throughout the book that relate to your experiences as well.

One of my first discoveries was that I didn't know what group of people I thought I belonged to. I never thought of belonging or not belonging to a group. Looking back, I noticed how my perception of myself differed from what others thought of me. How could it be that I saw myself differently from what others saw when they looked at me?

Many years ago, I had a minor parking accident in Switzerland. The other driver said to the police, "I

Lessons Learned

didn't know she spoke German." *What else would I speak?* I thought. I lived in the German-speaking part of Switzerland and it was my native language.

I remember one other day at the NYC Athletic Club, where I was teaching yoga, people acted surprised when I told them that I was from Switzerland because I didn't look like a "typical" Swiss person. I didn't think anything of it.

In addition, having been given an uncommon name like Raditia, I became used to being different and coming up with explanations about my name. What does it mean? Where is it from? And even if it is mispronounced, I don't think anything of it because those questions and inaccuracy don't offend me.

In the DEIA program of my mindfulness training, I learned that we grow up with a particular way of seeing the world, and as long as it doesn't bother us, we don't think twice as to whether that perspective is correct. What I am learning now is that there are other people involved in certain situations, and it's necessary for us to talk about our differences. Not to make them stand out but to make our differences the norm so we create a more open-minded environment and don't fall into, "Oh, that's just how it is." We should not become afraid of discomfort when exploring and instead get to know more from and about one another. That's the best way to grow and make life worth living.

* * *

In the experiences of "Lessons Learned," the focus is on my relationships, not only in loving relationships but also in friendships.

In some of my recent friendships, I have felt unheard and unseen. Yes, people were listening, though it felt like they were interested in something other than discovering if there was more to my concerns and sharings. I missed their engagement with what I was sharing. Over the years, I have learned that if I don't mention the thoughts that are going through my head, how would the other person know how I felt? How would I establish a more profound relationship if I kept significant pieces of the relationship to myself? I've been thinking about this missing piece of building a deeper connection with one another.

Lessons Learned

I have been practicing the concept that what I share comes from my personal experience and not as blame. It takes the courage to speak up and be honest. No matter how kind we want to be with our comments, when we bring up something that involves the person across from us, we will find ourselves in a challenging situation. Who knows what this person has just been through themselves? Who knows if they had a good night's sleep and ate well? And who knows if they disagree with what we are about to share? So many unknowns, and yet, we can't get around it mentioning what's on our mind at some point because otherwise, those thoughts will affect the relationship every time we meet.

For example, our feelings may be hurt because a friend is late or when two people gossiping about another friend makes us feel uncomfortable. Soon we arrive at the moment of truth; it never happens at a perfect time. We spill our thoughts and step into unknown territory. What happens then depends on three main factors:

1. How we present our thoughts (with "I"-statements, without blame and judgment).

2. What state of mind/body the other person is in.
3. What their past experiences are with you and others.

Depending on these factors, the response we get is either verbal or non-verbal, or both. This will influence what happens after.

I usually like to solve problems right away. While I was growing up, as mentioned before, at times, I was challenged in my relationship with my parents. Conflicts didn't always have a positive outcome. The conflicts were short-lived and came to an abrupt halt as others weren't willing, able, or interested in holding these uncomfortable discussions. These experiences didn't hold me back from returning to uncomfortable situations and bringing up what was bothering me.

However, there were moments when I had to learn to get the timing right when addressing different situations. For example, in the peer group scenario a year ago, as much as I wanted to get the conflict resolved, talked out, and put the struggle

Lessons Learned

behind us, I had to respect and accept the other persons' decisions in choosing work and attending to their lives. So what solutions could I bring to myself?

There were options of reaching out to other friends, and then what? Complaining about this relationship, no, not an option. Distracting myself from social media and other non-benefiting activities only to avoid discomfort? No, also not a valuable option. The only option I found necessary and relevant was going into solitude. I had to figure out what I was missing, and I wanted to see what I could learn from this situation. It wasn't easy.

Sometimes I wanted to distract myself. I'd rather reach out to a friend to talk about the issue and my thoughts about it than sit in discomfort, sometimes with sadness and grief. Other times, I'd inquire "What is this situation trying to teach me?"

What I discovered was how essential solitude is.

Being in solitude—by ourselves with ourselves—can give us great input into what we love, what we dislike, and what gives us pain. Being in solitude, which can comprise different forms of silence and disconnection from the hustle and bustle of everyday life, taught me that we all go through life at different speeds, with different focuses, and cope with our challenges differently.

I have learned to love myself the way I am and not feel sorry for myself through shame or guilt.

Different things can help us overcome the loneliness and discomfort of not resolving the conflict immediately. For example, through painting, singing, dancing, reading, journaling, and yet the most beneficial one that will change how we explore life is with silence and meditation—letting all our emotions move through us without holding them back.

My most significant discovery was realizing that when we don't force an outcome or pressure ourselves to resolve a conflict, other things in life can flourish that didn't have space before. I discovered that I love people for who they are, not how they make me feel.

Even though Maya Angelou said, "At the end of the day, people won't remember what you said or did; they will remember how you made them feel," I

Lessons Learned

agree with those words when it comes to certain situations. When I think of situations in which people are in our life for a longer time and who might not always make us feel great, I choose to remember that how a person made me feel can be temporary.

We can't always be on our best behavior, giving others what they want and need. Sometimes, it is the moment to give time and attention to ourselves, not to depend on others. As I will explain later in the chapter entitled "Unconditional Love," we can find a way to be complete just the way we are, and everything else will add to our experience. The people we engage with complement our experience.

* * *

Sometimes, in those times of solitude, space, time, and realization, we are able to see why we were in a relationship in the first place. We might have moved into a new way of living. Things are always changing. We are expanding and growing with the people around us by keeping a door open for new possibilities.

Be Human, Be Happy, Be YOU!

And even as I share these experiences of conflicts with friends, peers, and family, I notice how my focus was on what wasn't working out instead of what was working.

While moving through these experiences, I realized that there was a group of friends I hadn't even connected with during the entire time, and it made me understand that I wasn't as alone as I thought. This timeout was here to recognize where others had shown up for me, which is a whole new lesson in and of itself. All of my relationships are based on open conversations, space for opinions and different perspectives, and above all, the appreciation for our connection.

With awareness and some time in solitude, we can discover incredible things about being human.

* * *

At the beginning of this book, I shared with you that I attended a 10-day silent retreat as a server and learned a lot about myself. Connecting my lessons learned in friendship, I learned so much being with twenty absolute strangers for ten days and working in

Lessons Learned

the kitchen together. It was the first time I was able to learn about people I didn't know and how they impacted me.

I chose to be a server because I wasn't able to start the course at the beginning. When I arrived two days later, everyone had already been oriented to the space and its schedule; it felt to me that they knew what they were doing. At first, it seemed that I was stepping on everyone's toes. Everything I touched seemed like someone else's task.

When I feel uncomfortable and new, I tend to pick up on something to do and go by how I do it, for example, washing the dishes my way, which I realized wasn't a good tendency. I quickly adjusted myself by keeping my recommendations to myself and started to ask questions instead.

As it turned out, I took over someone else's job of dishwashing the next day. This change of direction—asking questions—turned out to be a great choice as the person leaving appreciated my interest in his tasks and made him feel more comfortable departing.

Be Human, Be Happy, Be YOU!

Well, that wasn't the only lesson I learned being in that retreat.

For a few days, I had the opportunity to get used to my appointed responsibility: collecting and washing the dishes from breakfast, lunch, and dinner. It wasn't as labor-intensive of a task as it may sound, as the facility had a commercial dishwasher. Several days after the retreat began, two more people joined our crew. They contributed to my lessons learned, both for different reasons. One of them had tendencies similar to mine: he knew how to do things his way and the only way. I became aware of how it can feel when we don't seem to care about other people's opinions. Seeing what I did at first and how it came across, I was glad that I found a new way to approach the various tasks with curiosity.

At the end of the ten days, I mentioned to my co-worker how hard it was to get to know him, and yet, I was thankful that he came. To my "surprise," it didn't end with my gratitude. He, too, wanted to add his comments and pointed out that my challenges with him were my own self-reflections. And our discussion didn't stop there.

Lessons Learned

He wanted to ensure that I dig deeper into where my challenges with him arose and named different people who could have had a big impact on our lives. The first one he noted was my dad.

The server pointing toward my father struck a cord, especially after my dad's passing seven months earlier. Being in a 10-day retreat as a server, secluded from reality, meant my inner world became even more vulnerable and sensitive.

For the next few hours, I was paralyzed from the exchange between the other server and me. With such profound grief about my dad, I couldn't follow through with my responsibilities in the kitchen. I had to retreat into my room. Whenever I came into contact with others, I burst into tears. It was a moment I will never forget. I'm so thankful to the man who helped me grieve in this safe space. I was fortunate to have people who were supportive and caring about this experience. As hard as it was to go through it, it felt freeing. It allowed me to recognize that there is so much love we can experience, even in the moments that are so difficult to grasp.

Be Human, Be Happy, Be YOU!

What I learned and still am learning is that no matter whom we meet and what experiences we go through, there is always something to be thankful and grateful for and that we can learn from.

* * *

This chapter connected my personal life with my professional life and how they fit together. To complete my thoughts around education and relationships, the lessons learned have shown me that comfort won't get me—or you—there. It's essential to experience challenges and discomfort, as these lead us to the next level of understanding. As much knowledge we have gained and as many degrees or certifications we obtain, we never know it all. There are always new lessons to learn. The best lessons are those that come from the heart.

The more we know, the more difficult it becomes to think we don't know anything. We want to put our knowledge, experiences, ups and downs, and discoveries to use and help others. At the same time, there is only so much we can do to support others on their journey.

Lessons Learned

As long as I focus on my journey and be open-minded, keep my eyes open, and listen more, the greater the chance I have of enhancing my life with others; in all the different relationships; family, friends, pets, co-workers, and strangers.

My hope and belief are that we are moving in the right direction of understanding and acceptance as long as we are willing to let go, let be, and explore all the other nine attitudes of mindfulness. When you attend to the "11 Attitudes of Mindfulness," (see last chapter), you will find that all the others will be taken care of as well.

The thing about lessons learned is that there will always be new lessons. As long as we pay attention to what's happening inside and around us, we will never be bored, and the beauty is that we never outgrow ourselves. Life's lessons are boundless.

Mindful Being

This chapter shines a light on where my path in life has taken me. This particular part of my life brings my whole person together—all my passions, love, experiences, and interests. It's the pinnacle of what I discovered being human truly means. This work has helped me stay connected to myself and includes all the parts I didn't know could fit into my life, my profession, and to find true happiness.

Since I created Mindful Being in 2019, many things have come to my awareness.

When I started my business, I called it "Body, Mind, Soul." Unfortunately (or fortunately), the name was already taken when I wanted to make it an LLC, so Mindful Being was established.

This mindfulness journey led me to discover that some of us have a hard time living out our inner dreams and verbalizing our concerns and disagreements.

I have come to realize that the space I want to create for people is where all of our thoughts,

Be Human, Be Happy, Be You!

emotions, experiences, opinions, pains, and anything we bump up against can come forward. A space where we remove our safety jackets and put our weapons aside, become raw and vulnerable, and realize that we all have that soft spot deep inside our hearts. A place where our wounds, which is derived from the Latin noun *vulnus*,[1] will open up. Depending on how we can relate to our wounds and how we are willing to see and let them be seen, we can make an impact in our lives and how we live them. Being present in our lives is truly a place of acceptance and curiosity.

My journey of connecting body, mind, and soul began in 2010 when I first taught yoga in Central Park, at different facilities around NYC, and at my workplace. My physical yoga practice wasn't that disciplined, my interests tended more toward the whole body-and-mind space that I shifted my focus.

As you read previously, when my professional life took a turn and I lost my job, I decided to explore college. There I was led to an unknown world. My view on life and what I could do changed. Losing my job gave me a chance to look at my life

Mindful Being

and I got the opportunity to be myself to an even greater extent.

I started to see that the small steps I had taken over the past four decades didn't have a name or a specific direction. A path had been laid out in front of me without my knowing. The beauty of this acknowledgment was that my life is not about knowing. It was more about taking life by the heart and following through.

As I reflect on how life unfolds, I realize that life doesn't just happen. How I live my life means placing one foot in front of the other, staying aware, present, alert, being open to new lessons, and meeting new people. In addition, it also means deepening the private and professional relationships I already have, and most importantly: *being me.*

In 2017, I taught mindfulness once a month for about a year at my former boss' new company in Connecticut, a 90-minute drive each way. Talk about commitment! And that was just the beginning of my sharing the concept of mindfulness with others. Over the coming years, I found more spaces to raise

Be Human, Be Happy, Be You!

awareness around mindfulness at libraries, schools, organizations, and other small studios.

I was given the chance to see how impactful mindfulness can be and how we desperately need to connect in healthy ways—not only mentally but with our whole being.

Being with other people, learning about the possibilities we have in life, and realizing that mindfulness is that missing piece we need to fully live the life we have. I became passionate about bringing my discoveries to more people.

The foundation of mindfulness is only the beginning of what we can do as humans with the body and brain that we have available.

As I observe others, I feel we're giving up too soon, wanting life to be easy and putting in the least work possible. I do not feel most of us are experiencing life to the fullest. We seek shortcuts to reach excitement before surprises can happen. When we take the extra time and rest, we discover where life becomes exciting and beautiful.

It's hard to put it into words; we will feel it in our bones. It's when our whole body, including our

Mindful Being

nervous system, senses, and a deeper connection to our heart, makes us feel alive, not just in our heads or how we think about ourselves. The feeling happens when our whole body feels the jiggles.

I imagine life as I write this and how I feel about it, I sense a deep feeling of love coming over me. It's a feeling that brings tears to my eyes because I am not caught up in the thoughts of "what ifs," "could haves," "would haves," or "should haves."

Pure presence—the presence of what makes me *me* and how far I've come with all the choices I have made—is what I am now experiencing in this body, with everything that comes together in this moment. Everything I believe in is taken into consideration and included in this experience.

That's what I want you to feel: a sense of wholeness, without any piece left behind or out.

As I watch life unfold, living is not something we do or a pill we take to make life happen from one day to another. Being alive is a dedication and commitment to ourselves, and the awareness of knowing that this is the only life we get to live and not to make it dramatic, just truthful. Yes, there are things like paying the bills and attending to a job, yet worrying and stressing out about those things won't do the trick. We worry and stress out about too much stuff.

There is healthy worry and stress, and there is too much worry and stress. The big question is: *How do I reduce worry and stress healthily?*

Before we get to how to cope with our worries and stresses, it is helpful to bring a little attention to our inner world. I am focusing on our nervous system, senses, and brain, because to practice mindfulness, we need to include all of what makes up our being.

Let's bring some focus to those parts of our bodies as they are strongly connected. Most often, we solely focus on our brain and thoughts, which leads us to forget some important features of our physical makeup. The more we understand our inner world, the greater attention we pay to how our outside world affects our vulnerable parts, such as our emotions, perceptions, and points of view. Mainly because being human makes up more than solely our thoughts and brain. There is a nervous

Mindful Being

system that shares information throughout our bodies from all the sensations we receive. One way to practice the awareness of our bodies is through meditation.

Whenever the conversation around meditation arises, some of the first questions are: "How can I turn off my thoughts? How can I stop thinking? How long does it take to have a calmed mind?"

There is only two answers to those questions: "You can't." and "It depends." There is no time limit for getting rid of our thoughts or stop them all together.

The first thing to know is that our brains are like computers or machines that create endless thoughts throughout our entire lives. That's what our brain does, whether we want or don't want those thoughts. When we understand that our thoughts will be part of our experience, we realize there are a few things we can do to accept what's happening in and out of meditation:

- Noticing what they are, without judgment

Be Human, Be Happy, Be You!

- Let them be and go
- Focus on one of the thoughts
- Focus on our breath
- Focus on a body part
- Focus on one of our five senses
- Focus on the external world with open eyes and a sense of observation

Mindfulness is here to remind us that we are NOT our thoughts. What we are here to do is to practice our awareness of thoughts and make sure that we are not getting entangled in them and making them our reality.

Recognize that as easy as it was for those thoughts to arise, it's just as easy to create new thoughts and shift our attention to something else. When we look at the relationship between our heads and our bodies, it comes to about 1:8. Meaning our bodies,[2] depending on our height, are eight times the size of our heads. Thus the degree to which we focus on our minds and heads seems a little off.

Mindful Being

By demonstrating the following, I hope we start to realize how we neglect a huge part of our bodies' connection, not the ones we exercise and take care of separately, but those we disconnect from each other, such as our brains, our digestive and reproductive systems, and physical functions. We see them as separate entities. Even when we look at our bodies from a Western medicine perspective, we rarely integrate our human makeup as a whole. We must consult with ten different doctors to take care of the injury or pain we are experiencing. Instead, we need to view a malfunction somewhere in our bodies as an integral part, interconnected to our whole body.

I am not a doctor or someone who has the knowledge of how to dissect something, though I am here to help bring some awareness to ourselves so that we will consider all the parts and see how they all work together.

In addressing stress, the first internal system I want to discuss is the nervous system.

We have all heard about our nervous system[3] and that it's our command system that controls

Be Human, Be Happy, Be You!

movement, thoughts, and automatic responses from the world around us, including digestion, breathing, and sexual development. By listing the many things our nervous system communicates with, we recognize why it plays such an important role when talking about mindfulness.

In addition, when we were only embryos,[4] our outermost layer was the nervous system. All the stresses our birthmothers carried is transferred to us. Not only that, all the stresses and challenging experiences our grandparents, great-grandparents, and ancestors had to endure, from the Holocaust and slavery, as well as natural disasters—all those experiences have been carried through to us through the nervous system.

Later in life—as an adolescent, adult, parent, employee, employer, or entrepreneur—without knowing it, you might have acted up and out on something you didn't know why and how.

Looking at our nervous system alone, we can see how complex our experiences are today. We are intertwined within multiple layers of experiences, most of which we don't even remember or know anything about. This knowledge helps to understand the complexity, and instead of adding more stress and worries, we might want to take a break and let those internal stresses settle down.

We can simply choose a few topics that are impacted by our nervous system, such as thoughts, automatic responses, digestion, and breathing. These aspects of our bodies alone relate to how vital this system is and the importance of giving it some attention. We can learn how to regulate our nervous system through different practices, such as awareness, breathing, and meditation.

Why is it so challenging to pause, to let our experiences settle in, and to possibly see that what we are bothered by has nothing to do with the particular situation? In my experience, it's because we don't have time or take the time. We feel rushed and are unable to spend some time inquiring about our feelings, thoughts, and sensations. Everything happens so fast that we can't take a moment to breathe and make sense of what happened. Even if we do find a moment to rest and reflect, either an internal voice or someone around us will ask us to give an answer, decide, and pressure us to act.

It truly requires a lot of practice to be okay with that discomfort. The discomfort of not knowing an answer and not having an immediate response can make us feel incompetent and confused.

When we allow pressure to build up whenever we find ourselves in a situation where we are asked to make a decision—for example, in connection to a job, a move, a relationship, or anything that might determine the future of making a choice—our nervous system will keep track of our experiences. It will signal to the other parts of our bodies—thoughts, movement, digestion, breathing, and more—when we are okay and when we are not.

By practicing pausing, awareness, breathing, and other actions that regulate our nervous system, we can create new reminders for our bodies. The next time we get into a tough situation, we might not stay stuck in our amygdala—the part of the brain that triggers fight, flight, freeze, or faint mode in our mammal/reptilian brain—because we calm the nervous system down through slowing down, becoming aware, and breathing.

Mindful Being

By referring to our nervous system and a part of our brain, we quickly realize that our responses likely won't change by having the right tools and knowing how to use them, especially because being human is much more complex.

What I hope you take away from this book is to spend more time in our whole body-mind and become aware of our thoughts, emotions, and sensations, while still being aware of other people's experiences. These observations are not only an intellectual game, but rather a whole body-mind involvement.

Being human isn't a laid-back kind of experience—one and done. If you want to live your life fully, it takes more than knowing how to meet your financial needs and having a great time. That might sound disheartening—what I mean is that if we want to live fully and experience life like no one else, we want to get to know ourselves, our tendencies, habits, likes and dislikes, and the ability to change those if we are willing to.

In the past, during workshops, I used to spend a lot of time explaining brain function. More recently, however, I only spend a short period talking about some technical terms because I want to get away from our *thinking* and shift into *integrating our feelings with our thinking.*

For mindfulness to be successful and beneficial in our lives, we must start by connecting body and mind, which is much more complex than intellectualizing experiences.

To give some context as to how our brain works, here is a brief explanation: Our reactive brain, the amygdala,[5] initiates our actions. Depending on how much time we allow between the input and the followed output, we might not respond from our prefrontal cortex, the part of the brain that understands consequences and helps us with wiser choices.

We are trained to make sense of our actions, and often that's the furthest from the truth. What we experience in life happens in a way we have yet to learn more about. Often we don't know why we said what we said. And furthermore, we are still in the process of determining what we genuinely want.

When we are rushed and pressured into making a decision, we are being held back from how life

Mindful Being

happens. Words become tricky and using our intellect is only half the answer to being human. We are experiencing an internal conflict of our thoughts, emotions, and sensations. We have multiple thoughts, emotions, and sensations happening at the same time that might contradict each other, so we don't know what to do.

The easiest way to get out of this confusion is by listening to our intellect. Sometimes, that aspect is only here to protect us. It's here to ensure we're safe, and unless we are curious, brave, and willing to try something different, we won't find other ways to be safe and protected. Another reason how the "11 Attitudes of Mindfulness" can access new possibilities in life.

Sometimes it takes a *leap* of faith—or just a *step* of faith—that can take our life in a new direction. It might be a path that is fun, explorative, and full of discovery so that we allow ourselves to live life differently. By only adding awareness, we will live a new life already. We will see a new life unfolding. We start to notice when new flowers start to peek out, when flocks of birds are in our backyard, a person making a pleasant gesture. These observations can come up when we don't act on a thought we had and instead observe it.

Mindfulness can transform us within the life we are already living. How we live life got so significant in the past few years because we started to realize how we neglected our personal life experiences because all we focused on was work and professional success. Then all of a sudden, COVID made the world stand still. Many of us had no clue what to do with that silence and pause. Some of us enjoyed the instant solitude. Our brains got bored; they had to create new thoughts, thoughts that made us feel uncomfortable. For some, it was the opportunity of a lifetime because it allowed them to breathe with no questions asked.

And then the world started to move again, slowly at first, and then from one moment to the next, we found ourselves back in the previous old grind. Everything happened so quickly that for some, the pandemic was just a blur, already forgotten, to remember what it was like and what opportunities it gave us. Many of us fell right back into our old habits and tendencies.

Mindful Being

Then there was a small group of people looking to integrate what we learned during those years and make this life the best we ever lived. How can we move through our lives with ease while the world is back spinning at 200 miles per hour?

My answer is simple: practice awareness. Awareness in all there is. Awareness of our thoughts, awareness of our emotions, awareness of our sensations, and awareness of the people we meet.

This exploration of body and mind and how to practice awareness is where Mindful Being steps in. This journey provides you with more accessibility to yourself and the knowledge you possess, not by giving you more tools, tips, and tricks. Yes, the "11 Attitudes of Mindfulness" are some tools. The difference between tools that ask us to add something external, such as putting time aside to meditate, work out, or regulate our nervous system, adding one additional thought process and take immediate action, is that you can apply them immediately as they best fit you and your unique situation.

Why Mindful Being? This journey of mindfulness will guide you to yourself and bring you back

Be Human, Be Happy, Be YOU!

home, support you to be yourself everywhere you go, and remind you that you are already where you are supposed to be.

Endnotes

[1] www.merriam-webster.com/dictionary/vulnerable

[2] www.scientificamerican.com/article/human-body-ratios/

[3] https://my.clevelandclinic.org/health/articles/21202-nervous-system

[4] www.ncbi.nlm.nih.gov/books/NBK526024

[5] https://my.clevelandclinic.org/health/body/24894-amygdala

Unconditional Love

How does unconditional love fit here? Over the past few years, from 2020 through 2022, I created an annual Spiritpreneurship Summit.[1] I invited people I met online when the pandemic happened to discuss different topics around self-discovery and self-evolution. I build a small community of like-minded people and connected with people who, like me, had created their own businesses around what they felt was missing in the world. They felt passionate about specific issues and did not have the answers. They stayed curious and open-minded to new ideas and wished to make a difference, especially with this new experience called COVID.

We talked about how we see ourselves in our businesses and the ways we move through life and the people in it. This journey came to a hiatus when 2023 was on the horizon. My focus had changed and I noticed that life had gotten a new way of being. People I had connected with went in different directions and had their own new focuses. Looking back on these three years of connections, I noticed that every single person I brought to the Summit had fulfilled a sense of love toward themselves.

During the process of putting the Summit on hold, I also discovered that we need to pay more attention to how we relate to ourselves. I noticed that it's very difficult for us to love ourselves unconditionally.

Why is that? Why can't we love our "flaws" and mishaps as much as supporting others through difficult times? How can we be compassionate towards ourselves? What will it take to unconditionally love ourselves? Exploring unconditional love is another way in which being human and ourselves leads to happiness. This realization let me dive deeper into this subject and search for the answers to why it is so hard for us to practice unconditional love.

I might have found the answer.

We grow up under the guidance of our caregivers. For most of us, it was likely our parents. I use "parents" as a collective word with the understanding that some of us were raised by grandparents, aunts, uncles, foster parents, or other significant people who took care of us and guided us to become adult human beings.

As I looked at the pattern and journey from being a baby, a toddler, a child, then a teenager, to becoming an adolescent, it is evident that we move through various stages. Our first twelve years or so, we trust and create a deeper connection with the people who led the way for us. Often, they unconditionally love us. No matter what we did or went through during those years, they will always love us.

Then we become teenagers, and slowly, the dynamic changes. We start to be more independent. We find ourselves in power struggles with our parents and ourselves. Some of us might have lost touch with the direction we were heading.

Not only were we dealing with the mental changes and the awareness of who we were becoming—our own being—puberty also impacted us. It was a time that our bodies took us on a ride and entered new territory. It was a time we had no clue what to do and were unsure if we wanted the help of our parents or not. We were in an internal conflict.

In addition, everything we knew was transformed into new shape in how we related to ourselves and the people around us. We were internally confused, and on top of that, our parents struggled with how to be supportive and give us enough space while unconditionally loving us.

Transitioning to become an adult is where the real journey of being human begins. Not only for us as teenagers but especially for our parents, who then were asked to be more open than ever, to move through discomfort with more ease. Then they found themselves in what we also call a "midlife crisis." These life changes are the ever-changing foundation upon which our humanness is built.

As teenagers, we found ourselves overwhelmed, uncertain, and confused while still being infinitely curious.

Where could we find support? Who could we turn to? Who understands us? Who's been here before? And who's willing to listen?

Again, our prefrontal cortex, the part of our brain that helps us understand complex scenarios and

Unconditional Love

can make sense of consequences, has yet to be fully evolved. We found ourselves when everything—our brain, our body, the extent of our knowledge, our idea of living, and how to function in this world—is still expanding, and support and strength are only partially available.

In this discussion of unconditional love, our parents' focus at that point isn't so much on teaching us about love and more about how to make it through school, how to keep our heads in the game and hope for a great future. What can happen is that we grow up, move out of the comfort of our homes, and are clueless about how to love ourselves—let alone how to love someone else, at least to the extent we want and can.

However, humans have an innate need for love. There is a missing piece that was freely given by our parents—being loved—that we no longer need in the way we received it when we were little. Now, we must figure out that gap on our own and fill it. We go out into this big wide world called reality, where we meet an infinite amount of people and come across an infinite number of ways to find love, either

Be Human, Be Happy, Be You!

through friends, work, school, or other people who represent a caretaker figure. We are blinded by what we truly want, which is to be loved unconditionally.

We might find ourselves in a loving relationship in our teens or early twenties. This new experience of becoming ourselves could cause us to feel inadequate in who we are, and chances are that we will subconsciously look for safety in someone or something else. The worth we see in ourselves will depend on and relate to those with whom we surround ourselves with the work we do, and especially how becoming of age was reflected from our parents.

Now what does the representation of living mean for us? What does this mean for life? And how will this affect our future selves?

There are many ways awareness can play out. One way is that we are unable to realize that the most important person is *ourself*, no matter what we do or who we are with. We will never be happy because the constant that is *us* hasn't been a focus. Even if we change everything around us, we will never be satisfied unless we genuinely love ourselves unconditionally. It sounds so easy and maybe even

Unconditional Love

somewhat discouraging, and at the end of the day, I have found this to be the truth.

There is the other, more hopeful way. We can change how we relate to ourselves. We can start loving ourselves!

Loving ourselves won't happen overnight. It depends on where we are in our lives and how much we have practiced accepting and loving every part of ourselves.

There will always be moments we fall back to being unsure of ourselves, unable to accept certain parts of us. And when we look at all the aspects of life, from our parents, education, jobs, and types of training, through our loving relationships and children, we can make a change.

We can start by loving the easy parts of ourselves for now and moving forward, making any necessary adjustments to embrace our whole selves, including the parts we dislike. Of course, it's not easy to love the parts that make it hard to be with people in challenging times or how we cope with life. However, if we don't include the messy parts, we will always have missing pieces, and we will tend to seek love somewhere else. Being on the constant lookout for love will never bring us the true happiness we are looking for in the first place.

During this exploration of "Unconditional Love for Ourselves," I asked people how they related to this incentive of loving themselves unconditionally. The responses I received showed little support for themselves. The judgment and expectations we have of ourselves seem so suffocating. Where will they lead us? We use a lot of energy when we use harsh and unforgiving language towards ourselves.

Love doesn't use energy, especially when it's unconditional.

What does *unconditional* mean? We say it, and yet, how do we really define it for ourselves?

Simply put, *unconditional* means seeing each other without the condition of meeting expectations. It's giving freely without wanting anything in return.

How often do we practice *being unconditional?* Even though we love our children unconditionally, don't we also demonstrate that we expect them to fulfill our expectations? Isn't there a discrepancy between what we feel and what our actions say?

Unconditional Love

When we show our children, friends, partners, and co-workers that we all make mistakes, we are revealing that we aren't perfect and don't know all the answers. That could be where we can start when we want to practice unconditional love. By leading without expectations. By creating an environment that lets us all explore our way of seeing the world in an open and accepting way.

For me, it's been years, or maybe even decades, in which expectations have built up. It's almost not possible to imagine what it means to "lead without expectations." It almost feels like I am lost without them. Where will I end up if I don't have anything to expect?

There may be a truth to that question, and at the same time, it's the beginning of embracing the person I am in this moment. Giving grace, acknowledgment, love, care, and comfort to who I am in this moment, not who we were at the age of ten, or will be on our deathbed. What will it take for us to look into the mirror and say, "I love you just the way you are!"? Maybe you've been practicing. If you haven't practiced much, the word "but" might find its way into your thoughts. For example, "I love myself, but I wish I wouldn't take things so personally." Such negative self-talk reminds us that we haven't taken care of loving ourselves fully yet.

We want to be perfect. With that goal in mind, we underestimate the power these thoughts of perfection have in how we relate to other people, ourselves, and how they connect to these subconscious conversations.

What are these thoughts in the first place? I see them as *imaginary* thoughts. They don't necessarily represent the truth. There is a possibility that the opposite of our thoughts is true. What holds us back from believing that? Do we believe we become negligent of others' experiences if we think highly of ourselves? Do we believe that admitting we love ourselves will cause a disconnection between the people we love because we are not supposed to according to how society perceives loving ourselves. Although lately, we have gotten closer to acceptance of love for ourselves.

Of course, loving ourselves can cause some conflict within ourselves. This is when unconditional

Unconditional Love

love comes into play because it includes everything about us, the good, the bad, and the ugly. There are no limitations to who we are. We are not only made up of the parts that are exposed to the world, but also those we hide behind closed doors. I'm sure there are parts we would rather not share even with our loved ones.

As I write these words, I sense the discomfort of how we relate to the whole persons we are. And here comes honesty. Unconditional love toward ourselves shows us our true colors, all the colors. What world would we live in if we only had the best and prettiest parts of us? Where would we learn lessons on how to do things differently if everything was already perfect? Where and who would we be?

We seem to be aiming for something extraordinary to free us from our shackles, but we haven't discovered what that would be. We are searching for the miracle potion that lets us live in a fairytale world.

As amazing as the conclusions of Disney movies are, "and then they lived happily ever after," we come to believe that the only way we can be happy is when life is perfect. Because we believe there is a

Be Human, Be Happy, Be You!

potential we haven't reached yet, we might not be able to love ourselves unconditionally. There is this "something" we are not being.

Believe me, there is a way to find that everlasting love and a happy place. It does exist, just not the way it's been portrayed in movies, books, or billboards.

This happy place you're searching for is deep inside you. It might be buried beneath all the struggles you've been through as a little child, as a teenager, with your parents, a loved one, or a job. We get hurt, physically and emotionally. There is no escaping that fact of life.

What will come from those experiences when we avoid them or address them righteously is that we not only disconnect from other people, we most likely disconnect from ourselves, and it becomes more challenging to truly reach that happy place.

As much as we wish that there may be only one perspective, one answer that is possible—our lives and experiences bring many different perspectives, teachings, and circumstances. Life and being human are not math equations. 1+1 doesn't not equal 2.

Unconditional Love

Our experiences don't always add up. There are contradictions.

Let me give you an example. I had a fallout with a friend. We had been meeting online during the pandemic and would talk weekly. We connected and agreed on many subjects, philosophies, and perspectives in life. At times, I found myself getting slightly frustrated when what I said wasn't exactly understood as I meant it. On occasion, we had misunderstandings about the time we were to connect because we live in different time zones. I felt like the person didn't care, had no sense of what I was talking about and what scenario I was in.

At the same time, I felt that I was bringing up so much understanding and time to see my friend's perspectives and being there as she moved through one of the most challenging times in her life.

After a few disagreements with her, combined with my intense way of expressing my emotions, I realized I was no longer able to bring any compassion or understanding to our interactions. Several times, we tried to restart our friendship, but at some point, we couldn't move through the situations and we had to take a break from one another. Initially, it felt to me that we would never speak to one another again.

About six or more months later, her words came back to mind. I was reminded that the way she experienced me had some truth. I realized that as much as I brought understanding to her, I didn't allow her experience of me to take place. This situation taught me about true friendship and also how differences are here to help us move out of our own way.

It would have been easier for me to say, *"Whatever. Why does she matter? Let me move on with my life and see this friendship as a moment in time."* Funny enough, that year, I learned more about unconditional love than I ever had before.

Meanwhile, I discovered and started to understand what it meant to be loved unconditionally by my parents and friends. I had not been able to comprehend unconditional love fully until then. My parents and friends demonstrated to me that no matter what, they would love me. And not just me

Unconditional Love

but humanity and people as a whole for who they are and what they teach us.

That is ultimate love. Of course, there are times that we get angry or frustrated. We need to let people be people and help each other to accept that we all learn at different speeds. It has taken some time, but I have eventually learned to understand the concept of unconditional love.

As the end of the year neared, and I was thinking about a word of the year 2023 and the word "honesty" stuck with me. It became my mantra for this year. As I reflected on what honesty meant to me, I discovered that "unconditional love for myself" is what I wanted to focus on, which connected to the hiatus of the Summit.

By using honesty with myself as the foundation, I had the urge to pick up a conversation with my friend from the COVID days with whom I had had the falling out. I wanted to start afresh and use "honesty with myself" as a guide as to how I could meet this relationship with openness and the opportunity to learn more about myself.

This experience with my friend has also brought

to my awareness that we often just see one another as an equal part of an equation, like $1 + 1 = 2$.

What I learned is that as much as the equation might be true, we all have different histories and backgrounds that brought us to the present moment. Now I am able to meet in the space between us to create a new experience together, instead of sticking to my point of view. We practice unconditional love for us.

Loving myself cannot only happen through accepting and loving myself. It also requires me to invite outside perspectives into the equation. When we allow this to happen, we open up to others and ourselves at the same time and practice compassion.

When we expand the capacity of acceptance by inviting in other people's views, life becomes more joyful and doable. It doesn't put us into a box that limits us. We find tools and resources that help us cut a door and windows to let the light flow in and out. We also begin to live outside the box and integrate the limitations into our lives.

When we look at unconditional love, there are no rules and regulations. It's a space of openness, curiosity, and trust that everything will be okay. Not because life is perfect or the problems are never coming back. Rather, we have moved into a space of compassion and acceptance that there are some things we can change and others that, even if we tried, wouldn't bring the satisfaction we sought.

These thoughts bring me back to the experience I shared earlier—being a child. Knowing that we mattered but didn't receive the love and approval we wanted from our caregivers and parents in the way we anticipated and wished for.

* * *

Now, how do we move from being incomplete to being complete? It's not a 1-2-3 path that will resolve a void of love or another missing piece while growing up. Sometimes we need to go through turbulent experiences to better understand how to make improvements that stick. Even though going through conflicts might feel time-consuming and draining, at the end of the day, the energy and time that goes into resolving a conflict is still far less than if we had gone a more convenient route. Resolving a conflict will turn into fuel and energize us. It establishes a deeper

Be Human, Be Happy, Be You!

understanding of ourselves and the person before us, even if resolving a conflict could mean losing a relationship.

How does all this relate to unconditional love? If we work toward being complete on our own and everything else complements us, e.g., having the right relationship, a good job, a nice car, etc. Then we are building a foundation that the external experiences aren't the focal point of who we are, but rather, our inner world is.

Once we make the connection that however we relate to our inner world is how the external world reflects on us, we realize that the only thing that really exists is what we experience internally. Observe yourself when you see a person who just frustrates you. If you are deeply honest with yourself, do you recognize that the thing about that person that gets you is something you don't like about yourself?

Here's another example. What do you look at first when you look in a full-length mirror? What are you judging? When you look at other people, isn't the thing you are judging the very first thing you look at? If not, you're ahead of the game. The people before

Unconditional Love

us are solely a reflection of who we are and who we see. It might sound unbelievable, but it's true. All the people we see and meet do not really exist in the way we believe they do, because what we know and experience cannot be exactly shared and experienced with anyone else. Whatever we share is being translated and understood only as much as we have experienced and comprehended it ourselves in our lives.

When it comes to unconditional love for ourselves, looking in the mirror can become effortless. There are ways to practice this. One way is looking into our mirror, writing down what we see without judgment, reflecting on what happened in the past, how our habits worked, where our challenges were, and then evaluate, make a choice, and act.

We only learn by trying things out, like raising children. If those methods don't work, we go back to the drawing board and:

1. Write down your observations without judgment,
2. Reflect,

Be Human, Be Happy, Be You!

3. Evaluate,
4. Make a choice,
5. Act, and
6. Repeat

* * *

The most significant aspect of unconditional love for ourselves is that we accept and invite all parts of us. We don't allow only feel-good pieces. We also include the parts that hurt, make us feel uncomfortable, and make us feel guilty.

There are two perspectives I would like to talk about. First is our use of words and second is how we connect to them.

Some words can feel powerful—for example, guilt. The only power there is, is the power we give that word. If we let guilt take over, and we start having conversations with ourselves that tell us: "See, you shouldn't have done this or that." "Why can't you learn from your previous mistakes?" "When will you learn?" Then we give power to these questions, and we shouldn't be surprised when people around

Unconditional Love

us affirm that our decisions were unforgivable. When we act, share, and let our thoughts be known, we can move on, leave these unsupportive thoughts behind, and focus on more encouraging and productive thoughts.

Let's take a brief look at guilt. That is one of the most powerful words that holds us back from experiencing unconditional love. My practice around guilt is to let it go. Personally, I don't believe that guilt supports our decisions and what we supposedly are "guilty of." Guilt shows up when we don't want to disappoint or hurt others. Our focus is external. When we connect to why we did what we did, and what we believe is the best choice for the moment, I don't think there is any reason to feel guilty if I truly believe what was said and done. If we can't let go of guilt, then that might indicate that we don't trust our decisions.

How we relate to what's happening within and around us depends on our comfort in our situation. Sometimes, we feel complete when we address the issues. Some of us prefer to deal with them internally.

Be Human, Be Happy, Be You!

Dealing with our struggles also depends on our tendencies, how people around us deal with uncomfortable situations, and what works for us.

Where I began and have expanded on, is the foundation of being "honest with myself." There are a few aspects I'd love to share with you. First, I want to reiterate my belief: *Every encounter we have with someone else is an encounter with ourselves.*

When you describe a conflict to a friend or spouse, was there ever a time that you felt that they got it, and yet there is a fraction of what you were concerned about that they didn't fully understand? If yes, that proves that no one will ever understand us completely, which is why honesty with ourselves is so important.

Let's address a second aspect—the perspectives of positive and negative.

Even though some people might have an aversion to using the word negative, here is an explanation on why I believe negatives are necessary. When we look at positive and negative, we find direct relations to physics and mathematics. In both cases, they demonstrate that we need both. For example, in physics, batteries or power would not function if we only had positives. We need both forms of energy.

When we use mathematics—addition and subtraction—there is something to be added ("I want more of that"), and something to be removed ("I want less of this") without judging which one is better. Using addition or subtraction just depends on what the result is we're looking for.

I prefer using the terms "positive" and "negative" because one isn't better than the other—we need both to function.

I have one more example: Nature. Nature needs rain as much as it needs the sun. Nature wouldn't survive without one or the other, and more.

These examples are here so we don't judge our experiences according to how they make us feel, and we establish a new relationship with life because it allows us to see that we need both spectrums. Without acknowledging positives and negatives, we won't see the improvements we want to make in our lives. The more we embrace all there is in life, the easier it becomes to move through life.

Be Human, Be Happy, Be You!

Let's return to the topic of being honest with ourselves. We can further explore how including both and all sides to our experience and reflection can help us be more inviting and acceptant of who we are. Often, when it comes to honesty, we mainly refer to the parts that can be improved and what we aren't so fond of. What about the parts that work well and define us just as much? When we think about being honest with ourselves, those positive parts of us don't come to mind at first. As we practice unconditional love for ourselves, that's where it is best to start—the parts of us that make us us—and that provide us with a strong foundation to embrace everything about us.

In preparation for a talk and some workshop sessions, I asked participants to fill out a questionnaire, from which I received a handful of answers. This was done to get additional opinions on what's challenging around the topic of practicing unconditional love and how we move through it with ourselves. What becomes evident is that we don't always like what we see. We don't want to see the truth. Either because it hurts or it means there is work to be done. Allowing those experiences to be valid and knowing whether we are facing them or not is still there. Honesty helps us bring our hidden tendencies and behaviors to the surface, not let them linger in the unconscious, and let it do the work underneath the surface. Just because we don't attend to our internal world and our struggles doesn't mean they don't exist.

* * *

Make being honest with yourself a daily practice, with little things like "What do I see in the mirror?" We can become more familiar and honest with what's already there and find a way to see and take care of our struggles while we can, before they take care of us.

I've heard different people describe their experience of not dealing with their struggles early on and how for a long time, they were able to complete all the tasks that were asked of, at work, at home, and with friends. Then, all of a sudden, another life took over. They felt paralyzed, unable to attend to the smallest things in life. There were signs all along, yet they didn't take care of their daily overwhelm,

Be Human, Be Happy, Be You!

thinking: "It all is okay; I can do it." Until one day, they couldn't, and were forced to change and learn how to live a healthy and well-adjusted life. A restart was required in a way they didn't know how to or wanted to.

You might recall a situation or situations when you might have stretched yourself too thin. Yet, you didn't know when to put a stop to the stress and didn't know how to do less. Maybe people have even tried to help and make suggestions for a change, and it didn't ring a bell. It's like the saying: "It's hard to read the label from the inside."

When it comes to being honest with ourselves, we are asked to take inventory of our life. We don't have to start with the hard things. We can start with the most important relationship in our lives—ourselves—by asking the following questions:

1. What do I see when I look in the mirror?
2. Can I meet my mirrored reflection with no judgment?
3. Is this challenging? Why?

Unconditional Love

By answering these three questions, we can build a new relationship and foundation with ourselves. We begin to see what we are avoiding. We also might start seeing things we do love about ourselves. Things that are challenging to see and, at the same time, help us to understand that there is more to us than the eye can see.

This practice and exploration are the beginning of including all parts of us. If this exercise hasn't been on your to-do list yet, you might realize this will create a new relationship with yourself. One that isn't in competition with you, one that has a purpose of having a voice, and that life is working with you.

* * *

Why is seeing things from both sides—internal/external—so difficult? As we were growing up, the focus wasn't as much on "Who are you on the inside?" The focus was more about who we were in relation to the people around us.

Often, the way people related to me during a conflict wasn't always pleasant, and I had many questions about what I was doing wrong. It never occurred to me to ask, "What is actually going right?"

The missing question is not about my inability to see both sides; it's my inability to be human. Putting our attention on what' going well is not in our DNA; it's a learned practice.

You are likely aware that part of our brain that needs practice is what's known as a "reptilian brain," the third innermost part of the brain, the amygdala area. This is the oldest part of the brain and is responsible for a large part of our decision-making.[2] It controls the fight or flight response and lives by its own rules. It also operates at super-fast speeds.

Many attitudes of mindfulness, such as compassion, unconditional love, non-judgment, non-striving, and many other attitudes, some of which will be discussed in more depth in the next chapter, must be practiced until our responses become automated.

Looking back centuries, humans had more to worry and be physically cautious about survival than we do these days, but unfortunately, moving from reacting to responding isn't a 1-2-3 adjustment. It requires tremendous awareness and patience; neither quality is something we innately and subconsciously

Unconditional Love

can do. Understanding particular natural abilities and where we actively need to engage will help us make different choices in life. That starts with being honest with ourselves.

The practice of unconditional love for ourselves doesn't stop there. Once I am honest and see where I excel and where I'd like to improve, I must act if I seek to make a difference in my life. Unfortunately, this focus on being honest with myself is a continuous and everlasting journey and inquiry.

Yes, we can hope and pray, and our wishes and hard work can come true. At the same time, while we hope and pray, we can also try things out that might not work out right away but will lead us in a new direction. Time will tell if we need to make any adjustments to stay on course.

It would be nice if we could put the data into our brain-computer, and everything would figure itself out. Okay, let me think again. I might not like that at all—this thought sounds like AI to me.

Where would the human experience be? If everything we wanted in life—the house, the car, the relationship, and more—were on an ultimate high, would that even be sustainable? Would that fulfill our lives?

You might think so. I would miss the things that make us human—having emotions and going through new experiences. The ability to change our minds and get excited about things we didn't even know existed. And that's where honesty leads us.

The journey of discovery is moving into a place of the unknown, helping us expand who we are, the people we meet, and expand our experiences. The answers we are looking for, the solutions to our problems, and the next best thing, to me, aren't as much outside of ourselves as actually inside of us.

I understand that becoming aware of my tendencies and habits, embracing my positive and negative traits, and having deeper relationships with the people in my life won't pay my bills. (I won't get into the meaning of money and how it exists—that's a story to tell for another time.)

What I have come to realize is that when we build on our traits, habits, and relationships, there is a greater likelihood of getting into an environment

Unconditional Love

where people want to be supportive. Arriving at that place that's built on the foundation of honesty creates unconditional love within me. That's the big money in our body's bank.

With this awareness, we invite every single human being into a life experience with us. We won't be able to exclude other people's experiences, not to mention our own. When we are honest with ourselves and practice unconditional love, then we are able to see the whole experience of others and therefore become aware of them in our interaction.

I believe that unless I love myself unconditionally, I won't be at peace with myself or anyone else. Without peace within myself, the challenges I encounter will overpower my ability to get hold of what's going on with my emotions and thoughts. My appeal to you and others is to practice unconditional love toward ourselves. No parts excluded.

Here are a couple of questions to get you started:

1. What would it take to love me unconditionally?
2. What do I need/want/miss to be loved?

Be Human, Be Happy, Be You!

The second question is a particularly significant one. When we explore unconditional love for ourselves, we will discover that there are certain aspects we need, want, and miss from others. The answer doesn't lie in the other person. It's what we needed, wanted, and missed growing up. Unfortunately, those needs don't carry the same significance now as when we were growing up, nor can we recreate what we missed and how we didn't receive the love.

When I was younger, I wanted more love. I took other actions to give myself the appreciation and validation I thought was missing. When I became a parent myself, I realized that others, including our parents, will never completely satisfy our needs and wants. Then I started to ask myself, "How can we gain the parts we needed, wanted, and missed?" My realization was to love myself as I am in this moment. I needed to find a way to create a new relationship with what I am seeking that comes from within. If I keep chasing love outside of myself, I will never be happy, nor will I unconditionally love myself.

Unconditional Love

Others can complement me, not complete me. Another reason we find a way to make ourselves the most important thing in the room is because it's almost impossible to get all the love we want, need, and miss from others. Otherwise, we fall into the trap of always depending on others. What if they can't interact with us when we need them? What if they disappoint us because our expectations weren't met? Who will be hurt? We will be. This is why our relationship with ourselves is the most important one. Once we crack the code to give unconditional love to ourselves, including all our likes and dislikes, and appreciate all the things people admire about us, we can become whole people. We will have the chance to build relationships that will go beyond our imagination of what is possible, and we will lead with love every single time, towards every single one.

Endnotes

[1] www.mindfulbeingllc.com/summit

[2] https://hbr.org/2006/01/decisions-and-desire

11 Attitudes of Mindfulness

Throughout this book, the attitudes of mindfulness have been related to my own experiences and how using these attitudes can bring more ease into our lives. I would like to take the opportunity to go through each word to bring more depth to these attitudes and discuss ways in which you can incorporate them into your day-to-day life. In addition, I will share my own interpretation of each attitude and how I relate to them, which may differ from the way Christiane Wolf, MD, PhD and J. Greg Serpa, PhD have used them.

It isn't always easy to shift our perspectives. Some days, doing so becomes more accessible than other days, depending on our state of mind and state of body. Are we feeling good? Did we eat and drink enough? Did we get enough sleep? The more we can practice the attitudes of mindfulness and bring them into our daily activities, the easier it becomes to move from one state to another. We can practice sharing our perspectives with others so that we can become interested in new ways of seeing life. If nothing else, practicing the following eleven attitudes will certainly raise your awareness.

1. Curiosity
2. Kindness
3. Gratitude & Generosity
4. Acceptance
5. Non-judgment
6. Non-striving
7. Letting go and letting be
8. Patience
9. Humor
10. Trust
11. A Beginner's Mind

For example, we are having an overwhelming day, and in our minds, nothing seems to work out. Everything we touched went wrong and took additional time that we didn't have. At the end of the

11 Attitudes of Mindfulness

day, our energy is depleted, and all we want to do is hide in our room and stay there until the morning. Unfortunately, that isn't always possible because we have other people who depend on us and our help. What do we do? We have a few options:

- One option is to keep going and ignore our internal voices.
- Another option is to get help and rest and let everything go.
- Another is to get upset.
- Last and certainly not least is the option of picking one of the eleven attitudes and putting it to use.

Let me go through each attitude of mindfulness and provide a real-life example. I will relate how we can apply the separate attitudes and notice how they connect and interact with the other attitudes.

Be Human, Be Happy, Be YOU!

1. Curiosity

Curiosity is one of my favorite attitudes because it leads to endless opportunities. It might be an easy one, depending on the situation. For example, I have a plan, and I know exactly how I'd like to have something executed. However, I need someone else's help because I don't have the time to do it myself.

I could find myself in an involved discussion by telling the other person about how I want the plan completed. The other person keeps sharing how they want it done, and we end up going back and forth. Neither of us wants to give up our solution to the plan.

What I can bring is some **curiosity** as to how the other person would solve the plan. By listening fully from beginning to end and keeping an open mind, I might discover how their way of doing the task could get the same result and possibly even be a better way.

Once we let go of how we want XYZ to be, the energy of forcing our idea onto the other person lessens. We might feel lighter or relieved when we listen to what the other person has to offer. An

11 Attitudes of Mindfulness

aspect of their way of doing things could adjust how we would execute the plan next time or confirm that our way is still the way we prefer. **Curiosity** allows new possibilities to arise and open our horizons.

2. Kindness

Kindness is a common practice and falls into the compassionate and gentle way of resolving internal and/or external turmoil. If we have the capacity to be **kind** and find something about a person that could be challenging, **kindness** can help ease our hearts. The challenge might feel less resistant and more engaging.

Just like in the example given in the discussion of curiosity, when we bring awareness to how others want to execute a plan, we can also bring **kindness**. When we practice an attitude of **kindness** toward something we aren't so fond of or disagree on, it might take more work, yet **kindness** might offer the opportunity to find common ground. The practice of **kindness** has many positive traits. Not only will it release tension and conflict more smoothly, it will also help us to see the world more **kindly**.

3. Gratitude & Generosity

Gratitude and generosity are closely related to kindness, though there are a few more layers. When we look at what we are **grateful** for, for example, in a relationship or work, we can see the parts that make us enjoy and be with that person or work and increase the positive things in life.

Our brains are more prone to negative thoughts and don't need much practice going in that direction. **Gratitude**, on the other hand, is a practice. Once we get the hang of it, we can make it a daily practice.

For example, we can list as many as five or as little as one thing we are **grateful** for each day, and all of a sudden, we will discover more things we are **grateful** for throughout our days.

Generosity is an active expansion of **gratitude** and kindness toward others through words and actions. We can share how we are feeling about someone and be **generous** with our words, which then can lead the other person to appreciate themselves more and, in return, provide us with a **generous** gesture. Perhaps that is lending a helping hand or offering something else that goes beyond their usual expertise and support. Through **generosity**, people might remember our interaction longer because of unexpected moments.

We can start by practicing **gratitude and generosity** with things that come easy and are related to daily acts. Then, when we are more exposed to difficult situations, these traits have already been practiced and can make previously uncomfortable situations a more pleasant and acceptable experience.

4. Acceptance

First, what does **acceptance** mean in uncomfortable situations? It doesn't mean we agree with what was said and done. It means that we **accept** what has happened. Here's a little guidance on where to begin:

Set aside 30 seconds to really notice what is happening in your mind, body, and environment:

- Is there something overwhelming?
- Do you notice tension, ease, or is your mind all over the place?

- Is the turmoil caused by too much stuff going on?
- Maybe there is an unresolved situation?
- Maybe you didn't get enough sleep?
- Didn't eat well?
- Maybe you feel funky for no reason?
- Are you content?
- Or perhaps you are experiencing joy?

What we are doing is taking a moment to reflect and pause at what is present. We can even take a few deep breaths to come into the present moment. Once we are aware of what is going on in this moment, including our thoughts, sensations, and emotions, we can now practice **acceptance.**

Can I **accept** what is coming up in this moment of reflection? And is it possible that my answer will be: "No, I can't **accept** what is present."

You might be surprised by how many things you can **accept** simply by being present. If we can't

11 Attitudes of Mindfulness

accept the present moment and what is, then we might want to move to the next attitude.

Again, it's not about agreeing or liking what arises in you. The short pause is solely to **accept** that those experiences are happening within me right now.

When we can **accept** without judging or wishing the situation was different—just taking note of what is happening in and around us—we are already a step closer to presence and release of tension.

If you're reading this and you are taking a moment and practicing **acceptance** of the current situation, you might notice that you feel a different energy than before practicing **acceptance**. By **accepting** the present moment with all there is, ups and downs, likes and dislikes, you can move through the rest of the day with more grace and ease and be even more **accepting** of help that could release you from a full plate and an endless to-do list.

Be Human, Be Happy, Be YOU!

5. Non-judgment

There are certain times in our lives we find ourselves in judgment of other people, what they are wearing, what and how they are doing and saying things, and endless other ways to assess other people's way of being. At the same time, there are endless things we can judge about ourselves for doing or not doing certain things. How are we going to tackle this one?

First, we can accept that we all judge. And even if we do whatever it takes **not** to **judge**, there will be a day and time in our life when we will judge again. This attitude is not about avoiding judgment, but rather, to notice when we are judging and shifting how we look at the situation.

Let's use an example of judging how someone is driving their car. Most of us drive or at least have ridden in a car. And most of the time, we don't know the person in the other car. No matter what we say about that other person, they will probably not know we are doing so, so judging becomes easy.

You are driving down your street and you're not thinking of anything, or maybe you're singing along

11 Attitudes of Mindfulness

to your favorite song, when out of the blue, a car drives out in front of you. You might even have to suddenly hit the brakes. You might wonder, "What is wrong with that driver?" "How dare they drive out of the side road without looking?" The comments might go on.

Is it possible that you have cut someone off unintentionally in the past? Is it possible that there was a time in your life while driving a car when you might have done something that could have possibly annoyed another driver? Willing or unwillingly? Most likely.

When we judge other people, it usually is for moments or situations in which we could have been involved in the past. At this moment, we don't remember having done anything like that. Or we are paying so much attention to avoiding doing whatever that activity or statement is that we can't believe that others are doing it.

I begin practicing **non-judgment** by acknowledging what is happening, asking myself if I did this or something similar before. I realize that no one is perfect. I acknowledge that the moment caused me stress and that I am fine. I might even include some gratitude that the car and I are fine, and I am still safely on my way to my destination. The incident might have been a learning lesson to pay more attention.

One thing I've been practicing in this particular situation to avoid any judgment is to always expect that a car nearing the main street will be pulling out. This meant that I began to recognize that there were fewer moments in which someone pulled out in front of me than I thought.

6. Non-striving

Then there is the attitude of **non-striving**. This is one of the more difficult attitudes to explain and understand, especially in an environment in which great efforts are celebrated and success is something we crave.

There comes a moment in which we experience a yearning for a particular outcome. We want to earn a certain amount, maybe we want to reach a particular position, earn a degree, or know what kind

11 Attitudes of Mindfulness

of a relationship we seek. Something that will bring us peace of mind, validation, acknowledgment, and other ways we want to be recognized. To get there, we do anything to achieve that goal, from working extra hours to completing more courses, speaking with more people, and working on ourselves so much that all we can focus on is the end goal. As I write these words, I feel this yearning, almost grasping, a sense of anxiousness, and desire to get to the "end" result I am striving for.

Now, why **non-striving** as an attitude? You might think, "Isn't that how we get what we want?"

Yes and no. Yes, you will get there with determination and commitment. At the same time, what we're missing is what's happening right here in the moment, being present with what is.

Striving doesn't allow us to pause, to take care of ourselves in a way that will have long-lasting success. Once we earn the amount we are aiming for, or get the job we wanted, or have a relationship we have waited for, we want more. We will always strive for more and more.

When we practice **non-striving** while still keeping desires and hopes for the distant future, we can get to our goals more easily, without neglecting the significant people in our lives. Releasing striving brings more ease to our journey. And when we include all our experiences and possibilities, we can achieve much greater success than we could have imagined. By **non-striving**, we invite our life experiences and present moment into the success we are working toward and allow changing direction if the "end" goal has shifted.

7. Letting Go and Letting Be

After exploring the attitude of non-striving, we have reached the perfect place to introduce the practice of **letting go and letting be**. This is the attitude in which most people would like to get more practice.

While **letting go and letting be** is self-explanatory, it definitely takes work to do. One reason is that it requires us to be less focused on the outcome and fulfilled expectations. It asks us to let other ideas and perspectives be present.

11 Attitudes of Mindfulness

Let me describe **letting go** more in-depth first. As in non-striving, there are moments when we find ourselves grasping for a particular outcome. For instance, an outdoor event is planned and then the weather brings pouring rain that day. Or perhaps we're in a conflict and wish to reach common ground.

Instead of obsessing over what could have been if only it were sunny or forcing our understanding and belief onto the other person, where both of these could feel exhausting, forceful, unsettling, and unproductive, one way to move forward is by **letting go** of what could have been.

When we **let go** of expectations and wishful thinking, especially when it's impossible for our wishes to be granted.

The feeling of pressure releases because we are inviting what's possible—for example, finding a new venue or listening more closely for points of agreement with the other person. **Letting go** allows us to see new possibilities.

Letting be is very similar; the main difference is in the action. When we let go, we are more likely to move on to new possibilities. By **letting be**, we can also see new possibilities arising, but our focus is more on **letting** them **be** present in that moment. This action is closer to the earlier described attitude of acceptance. We are **letting be** by not trying to find another solution or other options but by **letting** what is coming up **be** present.

One reason I like to focus on **letting go and letting be** is that we allow the experience to be present, and by **letting go**, we can access new ways of pursuing another option. With the first example I shared, the event will still happen either today or in the future, depending on the possibilities. By **letting** it **be** that the weather is rainy and we're **letting go** by not discussing the what-ifs, we can decide if we want to do the event on another day or quickly find another location to celebrate.

When we look at a conflict, we can first **let** it **be** that we disagree. We acknowledge that we don't see eye to eye, and by **letting go**, we can then move on by listening to what is really important. Thus, we can find new possibilities in how we can get past the conflict and move forward together even if not all issues have been entirely resolved and agreed upon. All this can require a lot of patience because we might have to wait to find solutions.

8. Patience

Oh, **patience**. Haven't we been practicing **patience** all our lives? As early as we can remember? When we were babies, we would cry if we were hungry, thirsty, tired—you name it—and often, we wouldn't get what we wanted immediately.

Now decades into our lives, we probably still internally cry when we don't get food, drink, or rest when we most need it. All we are being told is to be **patient.** Not now. In a moment. It becomes tough to accept that our wishes are not fulfilled immediately.

There are numerous ways to practice **patience**.

One way to start is by releasing the need for instant gratification. We enjoy and appreciate the food, drink, or sleep much more when we can't have it whenever we want. Whatever we're yearning for becomes more extraordinary with time.

Be Human, Be Happy, Be YOU!

Life can feel more challenging when we think about **patience** as if something is being withheld from us. Instead, if we look at what else awaits us if we wait patiently. This could even be a practice for our children to appreciate. **Patience** could also mean waiting with a twist. Practicing **patience** allows us to see and discover something else while we wait. We can make the time between wanting something or someone to when our desired objects finally arrive more exceptional.

I see **patience** as a practice of being with what is. The difficulty I see with **patience** is that when a yearning arises in us, it may also be accompanied with a sense of grasping and wanting as described in the non-striving. When we accept and explore what discomfort we might experience and turn discomfort into curiosity, **patience** receives a different feel. The more we appreciate and practice **patience**, the less it will feel like an unwelcome guest and turn into a companion we want to be with. It becomes something that helps our experience to flourish and allow things to unfold in their own time.

11 Attitudes of Mindfulness

Practicing **patience** might possibly bring with it some additional perks that before "waiting," we could not even imagine.

Patience is another word for commitment and dedication. Imagine sitting in a restaurant and ordering one of your favorite meals you haven't had in a while. You are having a great time with your eating buddy and wait patiently. Then your tummy starts to growl; you get more uncomfortable. After all, you haven't eaten all day because you wanted to truly enjoy an extraordinary meal. Time goes by, and your food has still not arrived. After a while, you ask the server when the meals will come. The server assures you all is fine but will check in the kitchen.

When he returns, he apologizes, and tells you that for some reason, your order was overlooked and that the kitchen will speed up the order.

At that point, there aren't many options other than waiting or leaving. Once we decided to stay, we have the option to fill the time with complaints about the restaurant and angry discussions about how we would never come back and so on.

Another option would be to return to **patience** and continue our conversation with growling tummies.

The **patience** we practiced may not be returned immediately, but it can teach us that not all is lost. There are ways we are given the opportunity to make **patience** work for us. Sometimes, **patience** will even be rewarded with a free cup of coffee or delicious dessert. Even if that isn't enough to make up for the long wait, it can make being **patient** a little more sweet and rewarding.

9. Humor

Now let's take a look at **humor**. How can **humor** be of support when life isn't all roses? Not only does **humor** help us lift a dark mood, it also keeps us from not taking ourselves too seriously. Life is already so serious when we look at work, making a living, and even staying healthy. The thing is, approaching life with a serious attitude all the time will not prevent undesirable things from happening.

When we bring more lightness to life, our lives become more joyful.

11 Attitudes of Mindfulness

Humor doesn't mean making fun of someone or something, or being cruel. At times, we can allow a tricky situation to become more comical. We start seeing with a new set of eyes and realize that there are other sides to life as well.

Comedy can be a great start as long as it isn't at the expense of someone else's misfortune. That would add another layer to the experience. However, there are moments in life where **humor**, fun, and laughter provide easy access to lightening up the mood.

Expressing **humor** can take practice. Some of us are better at this than others. It also takes finesse and awareness to see when **humor** is appropriate and when we might want to choose a different attitude. This is why we have ten other ones to pick from that might be better suited, depending on the situation.

It took me a while to understand how to express **humor** and make light of a situation. Luckily, I married a jokester who allows me to practice laughing at myself and taught me the beauty of **humor** over time.

10. Trust

After reviewing and learning about the attitudes of mindfulness, we have established a certain **trust** that no matter what circumstances we find ourselves in, there is an attitude that can support us.

That's one way to see **trust** and how we can implement it as a result of all the different ways we experience a situation, a person, a thought. We have also established a certain degree of **trust** within ourselves and possibly within another person or a thing in our life. What if we haven't built **trust** in someone, something, or ourselves?

Trust is a tricky attitude because we don't only apply it to a situation. **Trust** also has to come from within. When you **trust** enough, you will be gifted with a positive surprise. There are more layers that lead to **trust.** There is a sense of reliability, honesty, belief, hope, and certainty, that leads to **trust.**

Let's start with those. These characteristics must be established at some point for **trust** to fully exist. This doesn't mean that we need to be fully reliable, honest, believing, and hopeful all the time, though

11 Attitudes of Mindfulness

the more those traits are expressed, the greater **trust** we will have in what we do and encounter, including ourselves.

Often, we see the connections to **trust**, and even unconditional love, as something outside of ourselves, meaning we want to **trust** and love others before ourselves. To me, tremendous success and outcomes arrive when I fully **trust** and love myself. Not only will co-dependency of **trust** be reduced, **trust** also allows me to establish a stronger relationship with myself and enhance my relationships with others. **Trust** will expand when the values in relationships are met.

Let's use the example of **trust** in a relationship. If I **trust** myself to be utterly devoted to myself and then to another person, if that **trust** is broken at any given point, I still **trust** myself and that can't be broken. If we build on **trust** with another person first, chances are we will be disappointed. We get hurt or offended because the **trust** in ourselves isn't there.

When I build **trust** within myself, and I **trust** my actions, believing that all will work out, no matter what happens with another person, I still have the relationship with myself. Of course, the relationship with ourselves doesn't replace our relationships with other people. Creating this connection with ourselves is just a step that can help us maintain **trust** in ourselves when external events disappoint us.

This attitude is more about **trust** in myself than in others. How do I show up in a specific situation? How do I meet a friend in trouble? How do I also care for my needs that might need extra attention. How can **trust** be an attitude I can add to my life?

Trust is built over time and through many experiences in which the outcome might not be what we expected, and yet, it was a good and sometimes an even more excellent result than we anticipated.

Trust doesn't show its beauty right off the bat, like kindness does. **Trust** is more layered and complex, and when we are dedicated and committed to ourselves and other people in our lives, chances are our **trust** gets more beneficial and reliable. Once **trust** is established and expanded, and we have a track record of **trusting** our experiences, we can move into the last attitude.

11 Attitudes of Mindfulness

11. A Beginner's Mind

A beginner's mind is comprised of our minds, thoughts, tendencies, and habits that will, with patience, rediscover something different. By doing something we've been so trained and conditioned to do and give it a try to do it differently than we have at first.

The most straightforward example of **a beginner's mind** is teaching children something that you've been doing for decades, such as getting dressed. I am sure you have experienced frustration, and you'd rather do the task yourself because it will be much faster and exactly how you want it. Then you remember—children need to learn how to do the task because they will need to do it by themselves at some point. We could stay frustrated whenever we teach them a new skill or let them know what to do differently and how we do it together.

We have options. We could force ourselves on our children and make sure they do as told, OR we observe and look at what they are doing, seeing their choices, and how their brain works. Every brain works differently, no matter if we're talking to a child, an adolescent, or an adult. Regardless of their expertise and knowledge of what we are teaching them, our brains are wired differently. It is time for **a beginner's mind** to step in.

Now is the moment when we allow new perspectives, experiences, and thought processes to enter into our awareness and presence. Sometimes, I notice that there is a slight resistance to want to understand and see how other people are doing the same thing, as described in "Lessons Learned" at the retreat, when I adapted to the way the dishes were washed.

When we let the children or anyone we're communicating with take over, and we feel a certain degree of resistance or uncertainty, instead of getting worked up, we can become aware of the discomfort even if we might say, "I told you so" when that something doesn't work out.

And then again, where is the fun when we already know all the answers and never get the opportunity to say, "Oh, you are right with this one." Or "I didn't know we could do it like that."

11 Attitudes of Mindfulness

A beginner's mind can really be a blessing in disguise. We might learn a new way of seeing things. What **a beginner's mind** helps us the most with is creating an open mind to something we thought we had the answers to. It's possible to build a stronger relationship by letting the other person guide us, specifically when it's with someone younger than us. That person is given the opportunity to be significant and also provide some input to something they might have never done before. The beauty of **a beginner's mind** is that we still have the capacity to learn and let other people bring meaning to our lives. And what better foundation to create this relationship with ourselves and the people in our lives?

* * *

Now that we have looked at every attitude, we will automatically take care of the others while attending to one of them—sometimes, even more than one. I received many questions about implementing them, and my answer is "However you see fit." You don't have to go in order.

Be Human, Be Happy, Be YOU!

These eleven attitudes are a way to find more ease when dealing with inconvenient situations. We can apply the attitudes as often or as little on a daily or situational basis. Start with one you feel called to practice, one in which you already had some practice. I don't recommend beginning with one you consider the most challenging because I would like you to be inspired and excited about exploring these attitudes.

Sometimes we get motivated and are ready to take on a new skill and tool. And like with any new habit or practice, the continuation and commitment to include these attitudes in our lives will fade unless we see some small success when starting out. Don't give up!

In my experience, most things I committed to started small. Whenever I felt ready to take on one more thing, I went for the next step.

These eleven attitudes also allow us to move back and forth between doing and leaving these attitudes without feeling discouraged that we didn't continue.

If you feel discouraged at any point, I recommend beginning with **kindness** toward yourself.

11 Attitudes of Mindfulness

Become **curious** about what happened, practice **gratitude** and **generosity** for how far you've come, and **accept** what you can and can't do now with **no judgment**. Through **non-striving**, you learn to **let** the situation you're in **go** and **be** and take things one day at a time while getting better with **patience.** The next thing you know, you will bring in **humor** and laugh about the fact that the situation was not that serious in the first place. You find the **trust** that no matter how long a sticky situation will last, **a beginner's mind** will always be by your side.

Conclusion

Writing this book has brought me much joy and sadness, hope and despair, love and confusion. There are always at least two sides to everything. If we don't like what's happening one way, let's look the other way and see what comes from that direction.

There is still much more to discover. Writing out my experiences and lessons learned excites me about what else will come. What else do I still need to recognize and acknowledge? It seems that the more I know, the less I know.

Being human is a layered and complex experience, physically and socially. Knowing and accepting this lets us be open to life as it appears without wasting too much energy in understanding our experiences.

The practice of mindfulness is not a task to take off our "to-do" list. It's a way of living. Living with curiosity, awe, and wonder about life and what else we have not seen, heard, learned, and experienced.

Be Human, Be Happy, Be YOU!

Also, incorporating the complexity of being human and how our brains and bodies provides us with so much information without interruption. The main practice of mindfulness stays in awareness of what input we receive and make conscious choices in how we want to respond to the internal signals and share them with our external world. We can never underestimate the value our senses bring and how caring for them makes life worth living while it's a choice. Let's not wait until we need to and take care of life-changing experiences.

I hope sharing some of my stories and life experiences with you has brought more attention and awareness about how your life is unfolding and providing options and alternatives while you move through life. I would love to hear what you take away from these messages and how life gives you the many beautiful surprises to enrich your life as you find lightness, freedom, and ease in who you are. While you start integrating mindfulness into your way of living, at the very least, bring a smile to your face whenever possible. That can go a long way!

Conclusion

Exploring my journey through mindfulness, I have discovered the beauty in being human, learning how to be happy, and always be true to who I am.

Acknowledgments

Everything I experienced in life thus far and described in this book wouldn't be possible without every person who has crossed my path.

The deepest gratitude to have the opportunity to live a life full of emotions and space to make mistakes goes out to Mère & Père. Your presence, resources, and life have allowed me to live this life. And all the untold lessons you taught and are still teaching me. I am so thankful to have been birthed on Planet Earth by you.

Fabian and your family provided me with an understanding of what family and the significance of love means. Thank you for being you and staying engaged with life and wanting to create a better future for your family.

An immense appreciation goes to Gabe. Without you, I wouldn't have found the path to mindfulness as a practice and necessity to embody my whole self. You supported me in all my endeavors and always believed in my mission and passion. You are here through thick and thin, through sickness and through health. I am incredibly grateful to have you by my side through all the dull and exciting moments.

My dear son Max, you have and will continue to provide me with new challenges to widen my horizons, reminding me of where I fall short in my practice. My love for you is limitless, and my dedication to this practice wouldn't have been as strong if it weren't for my love for you.

Peggy, you represent love in humanity and teach me about caring for one another in a way I couldn't have learned any other way. Your openness, curiosity, and tremendous support in life and my journey have been profound. Thank you for your support in raising awareness with love and care towards one another.

Then there are my dear friends who I found online through the challenging times of COVID and have been on this mission to spread more love with their modalities, personalities, and ways of being. They have been an incredible boulder in the crazy journey of being an entrepreneur and guided by a mission of bringing humanity together. Thank you,

Acknowledgments

Swati Rohatgi, Eva Espinosa, Diana Venskyte Landborg, Kristina Crooks, and Lisa Kindle, for your uninterrupted support and lessons learned in making this mission a reality, supporting each other in believing in the bigger picture, and giving each other ideas and encouragement to continue our journeys.

A gigantic thank you to my rocks of friendship, Carmen, Silvia, Lorena, Sanna, and Kristina K., who have been there when I needed you. I know I can count on you when life hits, and all we want is to be heard even through the distance of an ocean. Thank you for giving your patience, friendship, and love to talk about life, odds and ends, relationships, and everything in between.

In my professional life, especially in the States, where the beginnings were rocky and my struggles of being myself and acknowledged were challenged, Melanie Fleiss and Attila Arian gave me the opportunities to make a mark in the professional realm in a new country where education has a different measure. Your incredible support over the years has built a confidence that would let me aim higher and for greater things. Also, meeting Kristina Biskup and

Be Human, Be Happy, Be YOU!

Michael Steinhülb in that environment helped me direct toward a US degree, which was a blessing in disguise. Having the opportunity to join Facade Tectonics Institute, a non-profit organization, twice has given me the privilege of working alongside Valerie Block, who supported my endeavors and provided an open ear and possibilities to spread the practice of mindfulness.

Having friends who trust and believe in you might not always be a given. It was Monique who got the ball rolling in where to begin my taking the next step in my mindfulness journey. Taking me to a workshop at school allowed me to put action into my greater mission. I am forever grateful for thinking of me and inviting me to join you. Having Monique, Avril, Sarah, Sara, Jen, Patti, Jane, Charu, and Mary in my life who supported me by listening and attending to my work have a special place in my heart.

My deep and heartfelt appreciation also goes to the wonderful people who brought my work to their spaces during private sessions and Talks & Meditations. A tremendous thank you to Monika, Christine, Sara, Kim, and Peggy for showing up and demonstrating that coming together in community and

Acknowledgments

being at peace, even if only for 60 to 90 minutes per week can make a difference in our lives.

A special thank you to Alexa Brandenberg from the Mt. Pleasant Library for continuing to put a word in to get my sessions going for the community. And I am grateful for meeting you, Liz Hammer and Lisa Breznak from the Hammond Museum; thank you for recognizing something worth sharing with your community.

Kira, my publisher, your kindness, tenderness, and professionalism are a pleasure to work with, and I can't wait to take the next steps to raise awareness in our communities and hearts. I am so glad Lisa has brought us together.

Last but not least, thank you to all the strangers who impacted my day-to-day life, from the clerk at the grocery store, at the post office, on the corner, and any other place we came into contact. This acknowledgment is here for us to recognize that everyone we meet, knowingly and unknowingly, is relevant to our lives. No one shall be passed by without a smile and a little hello. Thank you for being human.

Resources and Recommended Reading

10% Happier by Dan Harris

Altered Traits by Daniel Goleman and Richard Davidson

Atlas of the Heart by Brené Brown

Atomic Habits by James Clear

Change by Damon Centola

Choose Your Story, Change Your Life by Kindra Hall

Daring Greatly by Brené Brown

Decoding Greatness by Ron Friedman

Difficult Conversations: How to Discuss What Matters Most by Douglas Stone, Bruce Patton, and Sheila Heen

Generations by Jean M. Twenge, PhD

How Emotions Are Made by Lisa Barrett

How to See Yourself by Dalai Lama

Ikigai by Ken Mogi

In Love with the World by Yongey Mingyur Rinpoche

In Praise of Slowness by Carl Honoré

Love Notes for Life by Michael Cabuco

Love Your Enemies by Arthur C. Brooks

May I Be Happy by Cyndi Lee

Mindfulness in Action by Chögyam Trungpa

Moments of Mindfulness: Daily Inspiration by Thich Nhat Hanh

More Together Than Alone by Mark Nepo

One Second Ahead: Enhance Your Performance at Work by Rasmus Hougaard

Outliers: The Story of Success by Malcolm Gladwell

Principles by Ray Dalio

Psychology of the Media by David Giles

Rest in Resistance by Tricia Hersey

Sapiens: A Brief History of Humankind by Yuval Noah Harari

The Art of Living by Thich Nhat Hanh

Be Human, Be Happy, Be YOU!

The Dalai Lama: Freedom in Exile by Dalai Lama

The Developing Mind by Daniel J. Siegel

The Emotional Life of Your Brain by Richard J. Davidson

The Happiness Track by Emma Seppälä

The Hidden Life of Trees by Peter Wohlleben

The Inner Work of Racial Justice by Rhonda V. Magee

The Mindfulness in Plain English Collection by Bhante Gunaratana

The Miracle of Mindfulness by Thich Nhat Hanh

The Myth of Normal by Gabor Maté

The Origins of You by Vienna Pharaon

The Yoga Sutras of Patanjali by Sri Swami Satchidananda

Thirst: A Story of Redemption, Compassion, and a Mission to Bring Clean Water to the World by Scott Harrison

Understanding Our Mind by Thich Nhat Hanh

Why Good People Do Bad Things by Debbie Ford

Yoga: The Science of the Soul by Osho

Zen Habits by Leo Babauta

About the Author

Raditia was born to an Indonesian mother and a German father. She grew up in Switzerland and now works as a Mindfulness Teacher and Author in the United States

Throughout her life, she had the opportunity to be in touch with various cultures, religions, beliefs, and world views that supported her vision of the relevance of being human.

Curiosity about people and relationships has always been her passion. Her mission is to help people

Be Human, Be Happy, Be YOU!

find their way to being themselves while existing in social, relational, natural, and educational structures and limitations.

She believes the key to success in life is to be yourself and find a way to move with the complexity of being human and building deeper connections with one another.

mindfulbeingllc.com

www.ingramcontent.com/pod-product-compliance
Lightning Source LLC
Chambersburg PA
CBHW020926090426
42736CB00010B/1048